GED® Test

FOR DUMMIES®

A Wiley Brand

Quick Prep Edition

FOR DUMMIES®
A Wiley Brand

GED® Test

FOR

DUMMIES®

A Wiley Brand

Quick Prep Edition

by Murray Shukyn,
Dale E. Shuttleworth, PhD, and
Achim K. Krull, BA, MAT

FOR

DUMMIES®

A Wiley Brand

GED® Test For Dummies, Quick Prep Edition

Published by
John Wiley & Sons, Inc.,
111 River Street,
Hoboken, NJ 07030-5774,
www.wiley.com

Contents at a Glance

Table of Contents

Introduction

Perhaps you've applied for a job and have been refused an application because you don't have a high-school diploma or a General Educational Development (GED) diploma. Or maybe you were up for a promotion at work, but when your boss found out that you didn't finish high school, he said you weren't eligible for the new job. Maybe you've always wanted to go to college but couldn't even apply because the college of your choice requires a high-school diploma or equivalent (the GED diploma) for admission. Or perhaps your kids are just about to graduate from high school, and you're motivated to finish, too. Perhaps you just want to set a good example for them.

Whatever your reasons for wanting to earn a high-school diploma — whether we've mentioned them here or not — this book is for you. It gives you a quick look at the process of preparing to take the new computerized GED test — which, if you pass, offers you the equivalent of a high-school diploma without all the time-consuming bells and whistles of attending a high school.

About This Book

If you want a high-school diploma, you can always go back and finish high school the old-fashioned way. Of course, it may take you a few years, and you may have to quit your job to do it. Plus, you'd have to sit in a class with teenagers for eight or so hours a day (and probably be treated like one, too).

For most people, that situation doesn't sound too appealing. *GED Test For Dummies,* Quick Prep Edition, presents a different solution: Earn a high-school diploma and do so in the shortest time possible, without ever having to share a classroom with other people. If you don't mind preparing yourself for a series of challenging test sections that determine whether you've mastered key skills, you can get a GED diploma that's the equivalent of a high-school education — and you can do so in much less than four years.

If taking the GED test to earn your diploma sounds like a great idea to you, this book is a necessary study tool. It's a fun-filled and friendly instruction manual for succeeding on the new, all-computerized GED test. Use this book as your first stop. It isn't a subject-matter preparation book — that is, it doesn't take you through the basics of math and then progress into algebra, geometry, and so on. It does, however, prepare you for the GED test by giving you detailed information about each section, a full-length practice test for each section, and plenty of easy-to-understand answers and explanations for the test questions. After taking the practice test sections and going through the answers and explanations, you can determine which subject areas you need to work on.

Just as importantly, we walk you through how the GED test has changed. Although people needing special accommodations may still have access to the old paper-and-pencil test, for most, it now is offered only on a computer. Having basic computer knowledge is much more important. Some of the question formats have changed as well, so knowing how to use the computer mouse and keyboard to solve them is also important.

Foolish Assumptions

When we wrote this book, we made a few assumptions about you, dear reader. Here's who we think you are:

✔ You're serious about earning a high-school diploma or GED endorsement for existing qualifications as quickly as you can.

✔ You've made earning a high-school diploma and an endorsement a priority in your life because you want to advance in the workplace or move on to college.

✔ You're willing to give up some activities so you have the time to prepare, always keeping in mind your other responsibilities, too.

✔ You meet your state's requirements regarding age, residency, and the length of time since leaving school that make you eligible to take the GED test. (Double-check with your local GED test administrator to find out your state's requirements.)

✔ You have sufficient English language skills to handle the test.

✔ You want a fun and friendly guide that helps you achieve your goal.

If any of these descriptions sounds like you, welcome aboard. We've prepared an enjoyable tour of the GED test.

Icons Used in This Book

Icons — little pictures you see in the margins of this book — highlight bits of text that you want to pay special attention to. Here's what each one means:

Whenever we want to tell you a special trick or technique that can help you succeed on the GED test, we mark it with this icon. Keep an eye out for this guy.

This icon points out information you want to burn into your brain. Think of the text with this icon as the sort of stuff you'd tear out and put on a bulletin board or your refrigerator.

Take this icon seriously! Although the world won't end if you don't heed the advice next to this icon, the warnings are important to your success in preparing to take the GED test.

We use this icon to flag example questions that are much like what you can expect on the actual GED test. So if you just want to get familiar with the types of questions on the test, this icon is your guide.

Where to Go from Here

Some people like to read books from beginning to end. Others prefer to read only the specific information they need to know now. Chapter 1 starts off with an overview of the GED test and how to register for the exam. For those less comfortable with computers, Chapter 2 provides a lot more detail about the computerized GED test and what computer basics you need to know. If you want an overview of the different types of questions and how you can prepare for those subjects, check out Chapter 3. Chapter 4 gives you plenty of hands-on material to help you leading up to and the morning of test day, including what to do right before the test starts. The remaining chapters (Chapters 5 through 9) provide a full-length practice test for each section and detailed answer explanations. However you want to approach this book is fine with us — just don't peek at the practice test sections until the moment you're ready to take them (and be sure not to look at the answers until *after* you take the tests that go with them!).

Part I
Getting Started with the GED Test

In this part. . .

- ✔ Discover how the GED test and its various sections are organized and what to expect on the test. Get familiar with each section's specific focus and manner of dealing with the content.

- ✔ Explore the format of the computerized GED test, including how the questions are presented and how you're expected to answer them.

- ✔ Prepare for the actual test day, and find out what you should or shouldn't do on the day(s) before, the day of, and during the exam.

Chapter 1

Taking a Quick Glance at the GED Test

The GED test offers high-school dropouts, people who leave school early, and people who were educated outside the United States an opportunity to earn the equivalent of an American high-school diploma without the need for full-time attendance in either day or night school. The GED test is a recognized standard that makes securing a job or college placement easier.

The 2014 GED test has been completely revamped to bring it in line with Grade 12 standards in the United States. It also now meets the College and Career Readiness Standards for Adult Education. The GED test also covers the Common Core Standards, used by 46 states. These standards are based on the actual expectations stated by employers and postsecondary institutions.

The GED tests measure whether you understand what high-school seniors across the country are supposed to have learned before they graduate. Employers need better-educated employees. In addition, some colleges may be uncertain of the quality of foreign credentials. The GED diploma provides those assurances. When you pass these tests, you earn a high-school equivalency diploma. That can open many doors for you — perhaps doors that you don't even know exist at this point.

You may wonder why you should even bother taking the GED test and getting your GED diploma. People with high-school diplomas earn more and spend less time unemployed than people without. Some 59 percent of people with a GED were employed full-time or part-time, compared to only 49 percent without a high-school diploma. That result is virtually the same as people with a regular high-school diploma. Incomes were about 30 percent higher for GED graduates than people without high-school diplomas.

Ready to get started? This chapter gives you the basics of the GED test: how the test is now administered, what the test sections look like, how to schedule the test, including whether you're eligible, and how the scores are calculated (so you know what you need to pass).

What to Expect: The Testing Format Is New

A computer now administers the GED test. That means that all the questions appear on a computer screen, and you enter all your answers into a computer. You read, calculate, evaluate, analyze, and write everything on the computer. Even for work like rough math calculations or draft essay writing, you don't use paper. Instead, the test centers provide you with an erasable tablet. If you know how to use a computer and are comfortable with a keyboard and a mouse, you're ahead of the game. If not, practice your keyboarding. You at least need to get more comfortable with computers, even if that means taking a short course at a local learning emporium. In the case of the GED test, familiarity breeds comfort.

Under certain circumstances, as a special accommodation, the sections are available in booklet format. Check with the GED Testing Service to see what exceptions are acceptable.

The computer-based GED test allows for speedy detailed feedback on your performance. When you pass (yes, we said *when* and not *if,* because we believe in you), the GED Testing Service provides both a diploma and a detailed transcript of your scores, similar to what high-school graduates receive. They're now available online at www.gedtestingservice.com within a day of completing the test. You can then send your transcript and diploma to an employer or college. Doing so allows employers and colleges access to a detailed outline of your scores, achievement, and demonstrated skills and abilities. This outline is also a useful tool for you to review your progress. It highlights those areas where you did well and areas where you need further work. If you want to (or have to) retake the test, these results will provide a detailed guide to what you should work on to improve your scores. Requests for additional copies of transcripts are handled online and also are available within a day.

Reviewing the Test Sections

The GED test includes the following four sections, each of which you can take separately:

- ✔ Reasoning Through Language Arts
- ✔ Mathematical Reasoning
- ✔ Science
- ✔ Social Studies

You can take each of the four test sections separately, at different times, and in any order you want. This is one of the benefits of doing the test by computer. Because everyone is working individually on the various test sections rather than as a group exam, the computer-based test eliminates the need for the whole group of test-takers to work in tandem. For example, you may be working on the Math test, while your neighbor is working on the Social Studies test. Just don't look around at all your neighbors to verify this because proctors may think you're doing more than satisfying your curiousity.

The following sections offer a closer look into what the test sections cover and what you can expect.

Reasoning Through Language Arts section

The Reasoning Through Language Arts section is one long test that covers all the literacy components of the GED test. You have 150 minutes overall. However, the test is divided into three sections: first, 35 minutes on all content, then 45 minutes for the Extended Response (essay), followed by a 10-minute break, and then another 60 minutes for more general test items. Remember that the time for the Extended Response can't be used to work on the other questions in the test, nor can you use leftover time from the other sections on the Extended Response.

Here is what you can expect on the Reasoning Through Language Arts test:

- ✔ The literacy component testing asks you to correct text, respond to writings, and generally demonstrate a critical understanding of various passages. This includes demonstrating a command of proper grammar, punctuation, and spelling.

- ✔ The Extended Response item, also known as "the essay," examines your skills in organizing your thoughts and writing clearly. Your response will be based on two source text selections, drawing key elements from that material to prepare your essay.

  The essay is evaluated both on your interpretation of the source texts and the quality of your writing. You type on the computer, using a tool that resembles a word processor. It has neither a spell-checker nor a grammar-checker. You'll have an erasable tablet on which to prepare a draft before writing the final document. How well you use spelling and grammar as you write is also part of your evaluation.

- ✔ The scores from both components will be combined into one single score for Reasoning Through Language Arts.

The first part of this test consists of short-answer and multiple-choice questions (called items) in various formats. For example, they may be the familiar multiple-choice, drag-and-drop, fill-in-the-blanks, or hot-spot items. For details on the different question types, see Chapters 2 and 3.

These items are based on source texts, which are materials presented to you for your response. Some of this source material is nonfiction, from science and social studies content as well as from the workplace. Only 25 percent is based on literature. Here's a breakdown of the materials:

- ✔ **Workplace materials:** These include work-related letters, memos, and instructions that you may see on the job.

- ✔ **U.S. Founding Documents and documents that present part of the Great American Conversation:** These may include extracts from the Bill of Rights, the Constitution, and other historical documents. They also may include opinion pieces of relevant issues in American history and civics.

- ✔ **Informational works:** These include documents that present information (often dry and boring information), such as the instructional manual that tells you how to set the clock on your DVD player. They also include materials that you may find in history, social studies, or science books.

- ✔ **Literature:** Extracts from novels, plays, and similar materials.

You find a variety of types of problems in the Reasoning Through Language Arts section of the test, including the following:

- ✔ **Correction:** In these items, you're asked to correct sentences presented to you.

- ✔ **Revision:** In these items, you're presented with a sentence that has a word or phrase underlined. If the sentence needs a correction, one of the answer choices will be better than the words or phrase underlined. If no correction is needed, either one of the answer choices will be the same as the underlined portion, or one of the choices will be something like "no correction needed."

- ✔ **Construction shift:** In these types of problems, you have to correct a sentence by altering the sentence structure. The original sentence may not be completely wrong, but it can be improved with a little editing. In these cases, the question presents you with optional rewording or allows you to change the sentence order in a paragraph.

- ✔ **Text analysis:** These problems require you to read a passage and respond in some manner. It may be an analysis of the content, a critique of the style, review for biases or other influences, or responses to something in the content.

See Chapter 3 for the lowdown on this section of the test and Chapter 5 for a practice Reasoning Through Language Arts test, with answers and explanations in Chapter 9. Check out Chapter 2 for the format of the items as they appear on the computer.

Mathematical Reasoning section

The Mathematical Reasoning section tests mathematics that you'd normally know by the end of high school. Because this new test is designed to prepare you for both postsecondary education and employment, it has an emphasis on both workplace-related mathematics and academic mathematics. About 45 percent of the test is about quantitative problem solving, and the rest is about algebra.

The Mathematical Reasoning test consists of different formats of items. Because the GED test is now administered on the computer, the items take advantage of the power of the computer. Check out Chapters 2 and 3 for more information and a sneak peek of what the items look like.

Here are the types of items that you'll encounter in the Mathematical Reasoning section:

- **Multiple-choice:** Most of the items in the Mathematical Reasoning section are multiple-choice because this type of question is still one of the most used formats for standardized tests.

- **Drop-down:** This type of question is a form of multiple-choice in that you get a series of possible answers, one of which is correct. The only difference is that you see all the options at once within the text where it's to be used. For an example, see Chapters 2 and 3.

- **Fill-in-the-blank and hot-spot:** In these types of problems, you have to provide an answer. The fill-in-the-blank items are straightforward: You're asked for a very specific answer, either a number or one or two words, and you type the answer into the space provided. Hot-spot items use an embedded sensor within an image on the computer screen. You use the mouse to move data to that spot or plot data on a graphic. The secret of doing well on these questions is still to read them carefully and answer what is asked from the information given. These types of problems don't have any tricks, except the ones you may play on yourself by reading information into them that isn't there.

Some items may be stand-alone with only one question for each problem, or stimulus. Others may have multiple items based on a single stimulus. Each stimulus, no matter how many items are based on it, may be text, graphs, tables, or other representation of numbers, geometrical, or algebraic materials. Practice reading mathematical materials, and you should become familiar with the vocabulary of mathematics.

Science section

Our advice for the Science section is very similar to the Reasoning Through Language Arts section. Most importantly, read as much as you can, and read science material. Whenever you don't understand a word or concept, look it up in a dictionary or online. The items in the Science section assume a high-school level of science vocabulary.

You don't have to be a nuclear physicist to answer the items, but you should be familiar with the vocabulary normally understood by someone completing high school. Then read appropriate material that would be covered in high-school science texts. If you work at improving your scientific vocabulary, you should have little trouble with the Science section. (***Note:*** That same advice applies to all the GED test's sections. Improve your vocabulary in each subject, and you'll perform better.)

The Science section on the GED test concentrates on two main themes:

- ✔ Human health and living systems
- ✔ Energy and related systems

In addition, the content of the problems will focus on one of the following areas:

- ✔ **Physical science:** About 40 percent of this section focuses on physics and chemistry, including topics such as conservation, transformation, and flow of energy; work, motion, and forces; and chemical properties and reactions related to living systems.

- ✔ **Life science:** Another 40 percent of the Science section deals with life science, including biology and, more specifically, human body and health, relationship between life functions and energy intake, ecosystems, structure and function of life, and molecular basis for heredity and evolution.

- ✔ **Earth and space science:** This area makes up the remaining 20 percent of this section and includes astronomy — interaction between Earth's systems and living things, Earth and its system components and interactions, and structure and organization of the cosmos.

Go ahead and type in one of the three areas of content into your favorite search engine to find material to read. The search engine will give you links to articles and material from all different levels. Filter your choices by the level you want and need — for example, use keywords such as "scientific theories," "scientific discoveries," "scientific method," "human health," "living systems," "energy," "the universe," "organisms," and "geochemical systems" — and don't get discouraged if you can't understand technical material that one scientist wrote that only about three other scientists in the world can understand.

Items in the Science section are in multiple-choice, fill-in-the-blank, short-answer, hot-spot, and drop-down format. See the earlier sections on Reasoning Through Language Arts and Mathematical Reasoning for descriptions of these types of items.

Social Studies section

The Social Studies section of the GED test is scheduled for 90 minutes. Sixty-five minutes are allocated for the multiple-choice and short-answer questions, whereas the Extended Response item — an essay — takes 25 minutes. Here is a breakdown:

- ✔ **Multiple-choice and short-answer questions:** The short answers' source text and data will vary. About half of the questions are based on one source item, such as a graph or text, with one question. Other items have a single source item, such as a graph or text as the basis for several questions. In either case, you'll need to analyze and evaluate the content presented to you as part of the question. The test items evaluate your ability to answer questions, using reasoning and analysis skills. The information for the source materials comes from primary and secondary sources, both text and visual. That means you need to be able to "read" charts, tables, and graphs as well as standard text materials.

- ✔ **Extended Response:** Also known as the essay, this part of the Social Studies section requires similar skills and works much like the Reasoning Through Language Arts Extended Response (refer to the earlier section on Reasoning Through Language Arts). You're presented with one or two source texts, and your assignment is to evaluate the source text. You need to consider the quality of the argument(s) presented and then write an essay responding to and evaluating the opinions or information presented.

The content of this section is drawn from these four basic areas:

- ✔ **Civics and government:** The largest part (about 50 percent of the section) focuses on civics and government. The civics and government items of the test examine the development of democracy, from ancient times to modern days. Other topics include how civilizations change over time and respond to crises.

- ✔ **American history:** American history makes up 20 percent of the Social Studies section. It covers all topics from the pilgrims and early settlement to the Revolution, Civil War, World Wars I and II, Vietnam War, and current history — all of which involve the United States in one way or another.

- ✔ **Economics:** Economics make up about 15 percent of the section. The economics portion examines basic theories, such as supply and demand, the role of government policies in the economy, and macro- and microeconomic theory.

- ✔ **Geography and the world:** This area also makes up 15 percent of the section. The areas with which you need to become familiar are very topical: sustainability and environmental issues, population issues, and rural and urban settlement. Other topics include cultural diversity and migration and those issues that are of universal and not national concern.

It's a Date: Scheduling the Test

To take the GED test, you schedule it based on the available testing dates. Each state or local testing center sets its own schedule for the GED test, which means that your state decides how and when you take each portion of the test. It also determines how often you can retake a failed portion. Because a computer now administers the test, you can schedule an individual appointment. Your test starts when you start and ends when your allotted time is completed. The test centers are small computer labs, often containing no more than 15 seats, and actual testing facilities are located in many communities in your state.

You book your appointment through www.gedtestingservice.com. Your local GED test administrator can give you all the information you need about scheduling the test. In addition, local school districts and community colleges can provide information about local test centers in your area.

Sending a specific question or request to www.gedtestingservice.com may come with a charge for the service. To save money, you're better off asking a person at your local testing center. That way, you don't have to pay for the privilege of asking a question, and your answer will be based on rules and conditions in your area.

The following sections answer some questions you may have before you schedule your test date, including whether you're even eligible to take the test, when you can take the test, and how to sign up to take the test.

Discovering whether you're eligible

Before you schedule your test, make sure you meet the requirements to take the GED test. You're eligible to apply to take the GED test only if

- ✔ **You're not currently enrolled in a high school.** If you're currently enrolled in a high school, you're expected to complete your diploma there. The purpose of the GED test is to give people who aren't in high school a chance to get an equivalent high-school diploma.

- ✔ **You're not a high-school graduate.** If you're a high-school graduate, you should have a diploma, which means you don't need to take the GED test. However, you can use the GED to upgrade or update your skills and to prove that you're ready for further education and training.

- ✔ **You meet state requirements regarding age, residency, and the length of time since leaving high school.** Check with your local GED test administrator to determine your state's requirements concerning these criteria. Residency requirements are an issue, because you may have to take the test in a different jurisdiction, depending on how long you've lived at your present address.

Knowing when you can take the test

You can take the GED test when you're eligible and prepared. You can then apply to take the GED test as soon as you want. Just contact your local testing center or www.gedtestingservice.com for a test schedule. Pick a day (or days) that works for you.

Taking all four sections of the GED test together takes seven hours. Depending on your local testing center, you may have to take the complete test in one sitting. However, the test is now designed so that you can take each section when you're ready. In most areas, you can take the test sections one at a time, in the evening or on weekends, depending on the individual testing center. If you pass one test section, that section of the GED test is considered done, no matter how you do on the other tests. If you fail one section, you can retake that section of the test at any time. How the test is administered will vary from state to state, so check with www.gedtestingservice.com or your local high-school's guidance office.

Are special accommodations available?

If you need to complete the test on paper or have a disability that makes it impossible for you to use the computer, your needs can be accommodated. However, other specifics apply: Your choice of times and testing locations may be much more restricted, and times to complete a test may be extended. Remember also that if accommodation is required, the GED testing centers will ask for documentation of the nature of the accommodation required.

The GED testing centers make every effort to ensure that all qualified people have access to the tests. If you have a disability, you may not be able to register for the tests and take them the same week, but, with some advanced planning, you can probably take the tests when you're ready. Here's what you need to do:

- ✔ Check with your local testing center or check out www.gedtestingservice.com/testers/accommodations-for-disability.

- ✔ Contact the GED Testing Service or your local GED test center and explain your disability.

- ✔ Request any forms that you have to fill out for your special circumstances.

- ✔ Ensure that you have a recent diagnosis by a physician or other qualified professional.

- ✔ Complete all the proper forms and submit them with medical or professional diagnosis.

- ✔ Start planning early so that you're able to take the tests when you're ready.

Note that, regardless of your disability, you still have to be able to handle the mental and emotional demands of the test.

The GED Testing Service in Washington, D.C., defines specific disabilities, such as the following, for which it may make special accommodations, provided the disability severely limits your ability to perform essential skills required to pass the GED test:

- ✔ Medical disabilities, such as cerebral palsy, epilepsy, or blindness

- ✔ Emotional disabilities, such as schizophrenia, major depression, attention deficit disorder, or Tourette's syndrome

- ✔ Specific learning disabilities, including perceptual handicaps, brain injury, minimal brain dysfunction, dyslexia, and developmental aphasia

Because the test starts when you're ready and finishes when you have used up the allocated time, you can take it alone and don't have to depend on other people. For you, that means you may be able to find locations that offer the testing in evenings or weekends as well as during regular business hours. Even better, because you don't have to take the test with a group, you may be able to set an individual starting time that suits you.

If circumstances dictate that you must take the paper version of the test, you'll probably have to forgo the flexibility afforded by the computer. Check well in advance to see what the rules are for you.

You can also apply to take the test if you're not prepared, but if you do that, you don't stand a very good chance of passing. If you do need to retake any section of the test, use your time before your next test date to get ready. You can retake the test only three times, and, in most jurisdictions, taking the test costs money (check with your local testing center to find out specifics for your area). However, remember that you can take each section of the test separately, and each section is scored separately. If you fail one section of the test, like the Social Studies one, you need to redo only that section. To save time and money, prepare before you schedule the test. Refer to the later section "Knowing what to do if you score poorly on one or more tests" for details.

Signing up

When you're actually ready to sign up for the test, follow these steps:

1. **Contact your local GED test administrator or go to** www.gedtestingservice.com **to make sure you're eligible.**

   Refer to the earlier section "Discovering whether you're eligible" for some help.

2. **Ask the office for an application (if needed) or an appointment.**

3. **Complete the application (if needed).**

4. **Return the application to the proper office, with payment, if necessary.**

   The fees vary state by state, so contact your local administrator or testing site to find out what you have to pay to take the tests. In some states, if you fall into a low-income bracket, you can have the fees paid for you.

Note: You can also do all of this online, including submitting the payment, either with your computer, tablet, or smartphone. Go to www.gedtestingservice.com to start the process.

Never send cash by mail to pay for the GED test. Most local administrators have payment rules and don't accept cash.

Working with unusual circumstances

If you feel that you may have a special circumstance that prevents you from taking the GED test, contact the GED test administrator in your area. If, for example, the test is going to be held on your sabbath, the testing center may make special arrangements for you.

When applying for special circumstances, keep the following guidelines in mind:

- ✔ Document everything in your appeal for special consideration.

- ✔ Contact the GED test administrator in your area as early as you can.

- ✔ Be patient. Special arrangements can't be made overnight. The administrator often has to wait for a group with similar issues to gather so he can make arrangements for the entire group.

✔ Ask questions. Accommodations can be made if you ask. For example, special allowances include extended time for various disabilities, large print and Braille for visual impairments, and age (for those individuals older than 60 who feel they may have a learning disability).

Taking the GED Test When English Is Your Second Language

The good news is that English doesn't have to be your first language for you to take the GED test. The GED test is offered in English, Spanish, and French. If you want to take the test in Spanish or French, contact your local GED test administrator so you can apply.

If English, Spanish, or French isn't your first language, you must decide whether you can read and write English as well as or better than 40 percent of high-school graduates because you may be required to pass an English as a Second Language (ESL) placement test. If you write and read English well, prepare for and take the test (either in English or in Spanish or French). If you don't read or write English well, take additional classes to prepare yourself in English until you think you're ready. An English Language Proficiency Test (ELPT) is also available for people who completed their education in other countries. For more information about the language component of the GED tests, check out www.gedtestingservice.com/testers/special-test-editions.

In many ways, the GED test is like the TOEFL (the Test of English as a Foreign Language) comprehension tests. If you've completed the TOEFL tests with good grades, you're likely ready to take the GED test. If you haven't taken the TOEFL tests, enroll in a GED test preparation course to see whether you have difficulty understanding the subjects and skills assessed on the test. GED test courses provide you with some insight into your comprehension ability with a teacher to discuss your skills and struggles.

Websites that can help you plan to take the GED test

The Internet is a helpful and sometimes scary place. Some websites are there to help you in your GED test preparation, while others just want to sell you something. You have to be on alert to separate the good from the bad. Here are a couple of essential ones: Most are accessible through www.gedtestingservice.com.

✔ adulted.about.com/od/getting yourged/a/stateged.htm is a website that links to the GED test eligibility requirements and testing locations in your state.

✔ usaeducation.info/Tests/GED/ International-students.aspx is a site that explains GED test eligibility for foreign students.

If you're curious and want to see what's out there, type in "GED test" into any search engine and relax while you try to read about 22 million results, ranging from the helpful to the helpless. We suggest leaving this last activity until after you've passed the tests. As useful as the Internet can be, it still provides the opportunity to waste vast amounts of time. And right now, you need to spend your time preparing for the test — and leave the rest for after you get your diploma.

Eyeing What You Have to Score to Pass the GED Test

To pass, you need to score a minimum of 150 on each section of the test, and you must pass each section of the test to earn your GED diploma. If you achieve a passing score, congratulate yourself: You've scored better than at least 40 percent of today's high-school graduates, and you're now a graduate of the largest virtual school in the country. And if your marks are in the honors range, you're ready for college or career training.

Be aware that some colleges require scores higher than the minimum passing score. If you plan to apply to postsecondary schools or some other form of continuing education, check with their admissions office for the minimum scores they accept.

The following sections address a few more points you may want to know about how the GED tests are scored and what you can do if you score poorly on some or all of the tests.

Identifying how scores are determined

Correct answers may be worth one, two, or more points, depending on the item and the level of difficulty. The Extended Response (also known as "the essay") is scored separately. However, the Extended Response is only part of the Reasoning Through Language Arts and Social Studies tests. On each portion of the test, you must accumulate a minimum of 150 points.

Because you don't lose points for incorrect answers, make sure you answer all the items on each test. After all, a guessed answer can get you a point. Leaving an answer blank, on the other hand, gives you only a zero. Refer to Chapter 4 for some hints to help you narrow down your choices.

Knowing what to do if you score poorly on one or more tests

If you discover that your score is less than 150 on any section of the test, start planning to retake the test(s) — and make sure you leave plenty of time for additional studying and preparing.

As soon as possible after seeing your results, contact your local GED test administrator to find out the rules for retaking the failed section of the test. Some states may ask that you wait a certain amount of time. Some may ask that you attend a preparation course and show that you've completed it before you can take the GED test again. Some may charge you an additional fee. However, you need only retake those sections of the test that you failed. Any sections you pass are completed, and count toward your diploma. Furthermore, the detailed evaluation of your results will help you discover areas of weakness that need more work before redoing any portion of the test.

One advantage of taking the GED test on a computer is that you can receive, within a day, detailed feedback on how you did, which includes some specific recommendations of what you need to do to improve your scores.

No matter what score you receive on your first round of the section, don't be afraid to retake any section that you didn't pass. Now that you've taken it once, you know what you need to work on, and you know exactly what to expect on test day. Just take a deep breath, and get ready to prepare some more before you take your next round of tests.

Chapter 2

Examining the Ins and Outs of the New Computerized GED Test

. . . .

In This Chapter

▶ Grasping the essentials for the computerized GED test

▶ Knowing how to use the keyboard and mouse on the computerized GED test

▶ Familiarizing yourself with the specific types of questions as they appear on the computerized GED test

. . . .

The new GED test is offered only on a computer, which means that the test format looks quite different from the old paper version. No longer do you have to fill in little circles or use a pencil or scratchpad. Now everything is paperless, even the scratchpad of previous years has been upgraded to an erasable tablet. Now you enter all your answers into the computer. You use the keyboard to type your essay or the mouse to click on your answer choice.

This chapter provides what you need to know for using the computer to take the GED test and explains the different formats of questions on the GED test. We even throw in a few sample questions to ensure that you understand this important information. Demonstrating how to take a test on a computer with a printed book isn't easy, but this chapter includes several screenshots of question formats and other images you need to understand to be successful. All you have to do is read and digest it. We can't promise you a banquet of information, but this chapter is at least a satisfying meal to help you prepare for the next big step on your road to the future.

Familiarizing Yourself with the Computer

When taking the GED computerized test, you have two important tools to allow you to answer questions: the keyboard and the mouse. These two sections examine each of them in greater depth and explain exactly how you use them to complete the GED test. Make sure you understand the mechanics and use of the keyboard and mouse beforehand so you don't end up wasting valuable time trying to figure all of this stuff out on test day when you should be focused on answering the questions.

Because bundling the book with a computer would make it very expensive, we developed a different way for you to interact with the GED test questions in this book. We present items in a format somewhat similar to the computer screen for that type of question's format, and you mark your choice directly in the book. Then, you get to check your answer and read the answer explanation. Make sure you read the explanations even if you got the answer right because they give you additional information that may help with other questions later. That type of presentation may not be the most technologically savvy, but it does prepare you for the types of questions you'll encounter in the various sections of the GED test. For the practice test sections in Chapters 5 through 8, we provide a separate answer sheet for you to mark your answer. Then we give you the correct answer and detailed explanations in Chapter 9.

Using the keyboard

You need to have at least some familiarity with a computer's keyboard. If you constantly make typing errors or aren't familiar with the keyboard, you may be in trouble. The good news is that you don't have to be a keyboarding whiz. In fact, the behind-the-scenes GED people have shown through their research that even people with minimal keyboarding skills still have adequate time to complete the test.

On the GED test, you'll use the keyboard to type your answers in the essay (Extended Response) segments in the Reasoning Through Language Arts and the Social Studies sections and in the short-answer segment of the Science section. Although you may be familiar with typing by using one or two fingers on your smartphone or tablet, with the screen often predicting and suggesting words that you need with correctly spelled words, the word processor on the GED test for the Extended Response and short-answer sections has a bare minimum of features. It accepts keyboard entries, cuts, pastes, and copies, but no more. It doesn't have a grammar-checker or a spell-checker, so be careful with your keyboarding because spelling and grammatical errors are just that — errors.

If you're not familiar with the standard English keyboard (see Figure 2-1), take time to acquaint yourself with it before you take the GED test. Doing so is imperative because the GED test uses it. If you're used to other language keyboards, the English keyboard uses some letters and punctuation in different places. Before test day, practice using the English keyboard so that the differences in the keyboard don't throw you off the day of the test. You won't have time to figure out the keyboard while the clock is ticking.

Figure 2-1:
An example
standard
English
keyboard.

©John Wiley & Sons, Inc.

To complete the test in the required time, you should have

(A) comfortable running shoes

(B) minimal keyboarding skills

(C) really strong thumbs

(D) lots of coffee at your desk

Choice (B) is the correct answer. In preliminary testing, the GED test-makers and bigwigs found that test-takers with minimal keyboarding skills were able to complete the test in the time allotted. That doesn't mean that working on your keyboarding skills is a waste of time. The better these skills are, the faster you can type in answers, and the more time you'll have for the difficult questions.

You may want to wear comfortable running shoes, as Choice (A) suggests, but that in itself won't help you finish the test in the allotted time, although it may make you more comfortable sitting for all those hours. Choice (C) would be useful if you submitted your answers by texting, but on the GED computerized test, you have to use a traditional keyboard, which requires the use of your fingers and knowing which keys are where. Choice (D) may present you with a new set of problems. Computers and liquids don't go well together, and in most cases, the test centers don't let you take liquids into the test room.

You don't need to become a perfect typist, but you should at least be comfortable pecking away with a couple of fingers. If you want to improve your typing skills, search online in your favorite search engine with the keywords "free typing tutor." Any number of free programs can teach you basic typing skills. (Just know that some software may be free to try but then loaded with ads.)

When looking at the keyboard, you have to remember that

(A) All keyboards are the same.

(B) Keyboards from different countries have some letters in different locations.

(C) You should always use the space bar with your little finger.

(D) Touch typists don't have to worry about where the keys are located.

Choice (B) is correct. Keyboards from different countries have letters and punctuation in different locations and would present problems to touch typists who memorize the location of each letter so they don't have to look at the keyboard. Choices (A), (C), and (D) are wrong.

Utilizing the mouse

Most questions on the GED test require no more than the ability to use the mouse to point to a selection for your answer and then click on that item, which is very basic. If you're unfamiliar with computers, take time to become familiar with the mouse, including the clickable buttons and the scroll wheel. If the mouse has a scroll wheel, you can use it to move up or down through text or images. When you hold down the left button on the mouse, it highlights text as you drag the cursor across the screen, or you can "drag and drop" items on the screen, like you do when playing Solitaire on the computer.

On the GED test, you'll use the mouse to answer the three main question types: multiple-choice, fill-in-the-blank, and drag and drop. You'll use both the mouse and the keyboard to answer Extended Responses (the essays) and short answers. Refer to Chapter 1 for more basics about these types of problems. Here, we simply explain how to use your computer to solve them.

On the new series of GED tests, you indicate your choice of answer by

(A) using a pencil

(B) tapping the screen

(C) clicking the mouse

(D) yelling it out

The correct answer is Choice (C). For most questions (except the essays), the mouse is your best friend because you use it to indicate the correct answer. The present test computers don't have a touch screen. Tapping on them will only leave fingerprints, so Choice (B) is wrong. If you're going to use a pencil to indicate your answer (Choice [A]), you're taking the wrong version of the GED test or you'll look silly, trying to mark on the computer screen with a pencil. If you chose Choice (D), you'll, at a minimum, be ejected from the test site for being a nuisance and a possible cheater.

Fill-in-the-blanks are another type of question you'll encounter on the GED test. They're simply statements with a blank box in the text somewhere. To complete the sentence, you need to enter a word, name, or number. The statement will be preceded by directions setting up the text, so you'll know what is expected. Here's an example.

Type the appropriate word in the box.

The fill-in-the-blank question simply consists of a statement and a sentence with a 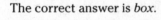 into which you type the appropriate text.

The correct answer is *box.*

You must type the precise word or number required. Spelling mistakes, misplaced decimals, and even wrong capitalization count as errors.

Getting more help with your computer skills

Some websites offer free training on basic computer skills, but you need a computer to use them. Your local library should have free computer access if you don't have your own. One website that offers good basic training is www.skillfunsenior.com/skills/mouse. Websites are transient, so if this one no longer functions, search online for other basic computer skill tutorials for a few more sites.

Take your time at home or in the library developing your skills and working through the practice tests. Test day isn't the time to figure out how to use the computer.

Try this question:

A good place to get help using a computer is

    (A) your local school

    (B) the Internet

    (C) libraries

    (D) all of the above

The correct answer is Choice (D). Any place that offers instruction in using a computer is a good place to go for help.

Recognizing What the Questions Look Like on the Computer Screen

As you take the computerized GED test, you'll encounter three main types of problems to solve: multiple-choice, fill-in-the-blank, and drag and drop. You may also have to deal with hot-spot questions and short-answer questions, depending on the test section. The hot spot is simply an area on the screen that reacts when you roll the mouse pointer over it. It appears mainly on the Mathematical Reasoning and Science tests, where it allows you to create graphs or charts.

The following sections show you what the different questions look like on the screen in the different test sections and explain how to answer these questions.

Reasoning Through Language Arts section

The Reasoning Through Language Arts section tests several skills, including reading and comprehension, grammar and spelling, and writing skills. Most of the content for answering literature and comprehension questions will be in the source text itself, but for grammar and spelling, you'll need to know the answers from your studying.

Multiple-choice questions

Like in all the four test sections, the multiple-choice question, or item, is the most popular. The basic multiple-choice question, as shown in Figure 2-2, looks very similar to what appeared in the print format of previous versions of the GED test. It's presented in split-screen form, with the source text on the left and the question and answer choices on the right. You read the question and the source text first and then answer the question. If the source text extends beyond one screen, you use the scroll bar on the right side of the left screen. When you're ready to answer, use the mouse to click on the appropriate answer, and then click on Next to continue.

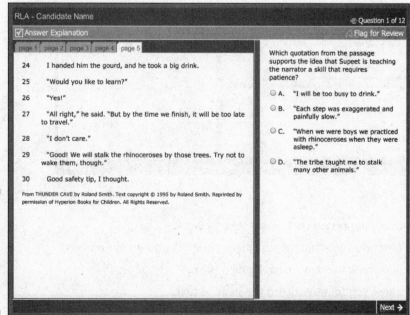

Figure 2-2: An example of a standard multiple-choice question.

If a scroll bar accompanies the source text on the left side of the screen, some of the text isn't visible unless you scroll down. If that scroll bar is on the answer side, some of the answer choices may not be visible without scrolling. This is important to remember because you may miss some important text when trying to answer the item.

The scroll bar in some items will help you

(A) Find scrolls.

(B) Move around the screen.

(C) Go on to the next question.

(D) Recognize that more text is above or below what is currently on the screen.

Choice (D) is correct. The scroll bar is simply a visual reminder that the text is longer than what's shown on the screen. It doesn't help you do anything else — not move around the screen, go to the next question, or find scrolls.

Sometimes the source text consists of several screen pages (see Figure 2-3). The tabs at the top of the page are your clue. They actually look like tabs on file folders. Each one opens the next page in the source text when you click on the tab. Remember that you must read all the text to be able to answer the question. Notice, too, that the question side of the screen doesn't change as you go through the tabs. Otherwise, it works the same way: read, decide on an answer, click on the matching choice, and then click on Next to continue.

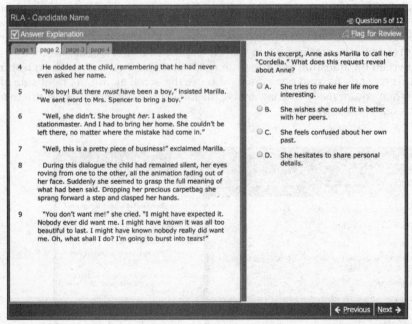

Figure 2-3:
An example of a multiple-choice question with tabs.

Copyright © 2014 GED Testing Service LLC

Tabs are a very important part of any item because

(A) They give you something to do while you think about your answer.

(B) They allow you to advance to the next page.

(C) They allow you to move down the page of text.

(D) It's the trade name for a diet cola from yesteryear.

Choice (B) is the correct answer. If you have to advance through a passage, the tabs give you the mechanism to do so. If you choose not to use the tabs, you'll be able to read only one page of the passage. Because the answer to the item is dependent on all the presented material, it puts you at a major disadvantage.

Most of the items on the test will be some form of multiple-choice, presented in a manner as the preceding two examples.

Drag-and-drop questions

The Reasoning Through Language Arts section also uses other question formats suited to computer testing. The drag-and-drop question (see Figure 2-4) is one variation. The source text, an excerpt from *Anne of Green Gables,* is on the left side of the screen.

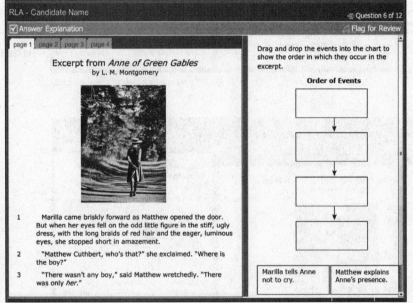

Figure 2-4: An example of a drag- and-drop question using boxes.

This question covers more than one page, accessible via the tabs. On the answer side, the scroll bar indicates that the content continues on, and you must scroll down to see it all (see Figure 2-5). When you scroll down, you can see the content you missed on the initial screen.

After you finish reading the content under all four tabs, drag the choices on the right into the boxes. You click on the item, and without letting go of the mouse button, you drag the item up to the correct box. Let go of the mouse and the item drops into the box. If you've moved it properly, it will stay where you dropped it.

Figure 2-6 shows another sample drag-and-drop problem. This question uses the same four-page source text and asks you to select characteristics that apply to Anne. The key is that you can select only three of the five listed words. That isn't stated in the question but is obvious from the drag-and-drop targets, which include only three spaces but have five options. You have to read the text carefully to find the correct choices. When you decide which words apply, drag each word to one of the drop targets and leave it there. Click on Next to continue.

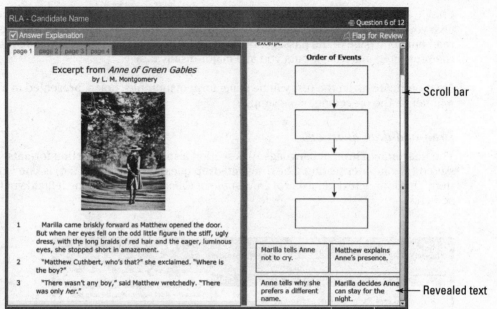

Figure 2-5:
Use the scroll bar to scroll down.

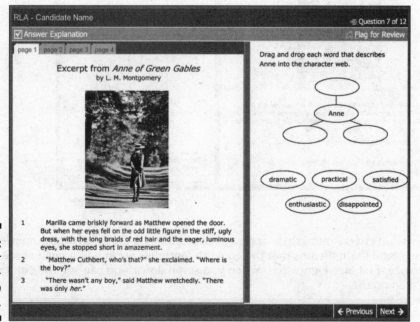

Figure 2-6:
Another drag-and-drop example.

In this book, you clearly can't drag and drop on the page, so for questions in this format, you'll indicate your answer on the answer sheet.

Answering a drag-and-drop question requires you to

(A) Move the computer desk to a new location.

(B) Type directly into a box.

(C) Click on and move an answer choice.

(D) Play yet another game of Scrabble.

Choice (C) is correct. Choice (A) refers more to rearranging furniture and not taking a test. Choice (B) refers to the directions for fill-in-the-blank, Extended Response, or short-answer items, and Choice (D) is a prescription for wasting time that could be better spent preparing for the test.

Drop-down menu questions

You'll also encounter other more technologically enhanced questions. One type asks you to correct, edit, or generally improve samples of writing. In Figure 2-7, the source text contains drop-down menus. In one line of the text, you see a blank space and the word *Select* . . . with an arrow next to it. When you click on that line, a number of variations appear. You pick the best choice as your answer.

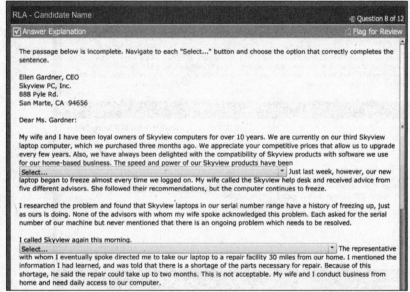

Figure 2-7: An example of a drop-down menu question.

Figure 2-8 shows what you see when you click on the Select line.

From the context of the letter in the item, you have to select the sentence that fits best and shows both correct grammar and correct spelling. Move the mouse to the proper choice and let go. The corrected wording will appear in the space. You can now read the entire text to review and decide whether you indeed selected the appropriate choice. Figure 2-9 is a close-up of one item where the drop-down menu asks you to choose only a single correct word.

For the purposes of this book, the drop-down menu questions look a lot like multiple-choice questions. We include a list of answer choices for you to choose from, labeled with A, B, C, and D. Just know that on the computerized GED test, you'll have to click on Select to view the answer choices.

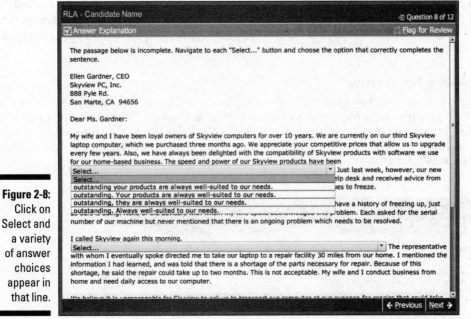

Figure 2-8: Click on Select and a variety of answer choices appear in that line.

Copyright © 2014 GED Testing Service LLC

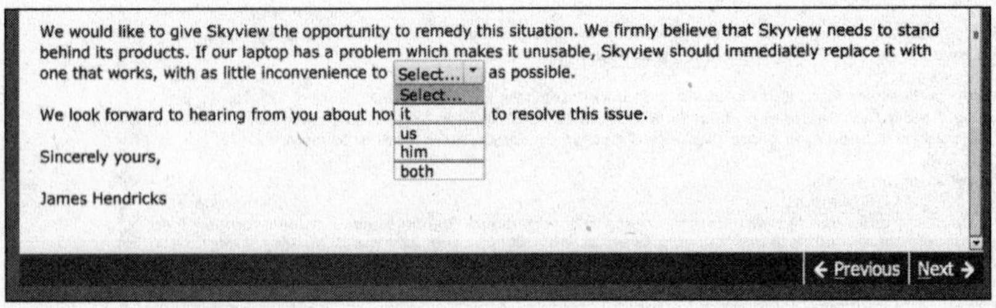

Figure 2-9: Another example of a drop-down menu question.

Copyright © 2014 GED Testing Service LLC

The Extended Response

In the Extended Response of the Reasoning Through Language Arts section, you get 45 minutes to write an essay. Figure 2-10 shows an example. Note that the source material is longer than one screen. The tabs on the top of the left side indicate that this text is spread out over four pages. Be sure to read all four pages with care. You'll have an erasable tablet to take notes and write drafts of your essay. Use it to make notes as you read.

The answer window is a mini word processor. In Figure 2-10, you can see that it allows you to cut, paste, copy, do, and undo. However, it doesn't have either a grammar-checker or a spell-checker. Your brain with its experience and knowledge supplies those. To copy, cut, paste, or save, you move the mouse cursor to the area of the screen with the symbols for performing these tasks, and then you click on a mouse button to activate the feature (or you can use the standard keyboard shortcuts for cut and paste). You'll use this feature primarily if you want to quote something in your essay.

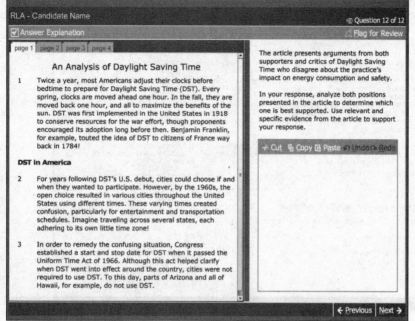

Answer Explanation   Flag for Review

page 1 page 2 page 3 page 4

An Analysis of Daylight Saving Time

1   Twice a year, most Americans adjust their clocks before bedtime to prepare for Daylight Saving Time (DST). Every spring, clocks are moved ahead one hour. In the fall, they are moved back one hour, and all to maximize the benefits of the sun. DST was first implemented in the United States in 1918 to conserve resources for the war effort, though proponents encouraged its adoption long before then. Benjamin Franklin, for example, touted the idea of DST to citizens of France way back in 1784!

DST in America

2   For years following DST's U.S. debut, cities could choose if and when they wanted to participate. However, by the 1960s, the open choice resulted in various cities throughout the United States using different times. These varying times created confusion, particularly for entertainment and transportation schedules. Imagine traveling across several states, each adhering to its own little time zone!

3   In order to remedy the confusing situation, Congress established a start and stop date for DST when it passed the Uniform Time Act of 1966. Although this act helped clarify when DST went into effect around the country, cities were not required to use DST. To this day, parts of Arizona and all of Hawaii, for example, do not use DST.

The article presents arguments from both supporters and critics of Daylight Saving Time who disagree about the practice's impact on energy consumption and safety.

In your response, analyze both positions presented in the article to determine which one is best supported. Use relevant and specific evidence from the article to support your response.

Cut   Copy   Paste   Undo   Redo

← Previous | Next →

Figure 2-10: A sample Reasoning Through Language Arts Extended Response.

Take a stab at writing a full-length essay in the practice test section in Chapter 5. Time the test so you're taking it under the same conditions as the real GED test.

Social Studies section

In the Social Studies section on the GED test, you'll encounter all the same types of questions as you do in the Reasoning Through Language Arts section. Here is a brief guide to the kinds of questions to expect.

Multiple-choice questions

Most questions on the Social Studies section are a variation of multiple-choice questions. You're probably most familiar with this simplest version (see Figure 2-11).

To answer this question, you click on the correct choice, and then click on Next to continue. (To answer this type of question in the book, you simply mark your choice of answer on an answer sheet, and then check your answer, read the explanation, and make sure you understand why you got the item right or wrong. You can often discover as much from getting an answer correct, and reading the explanation of why it's correct, as in getting it wrong.)

You'll also find the multiple-choice and other items presented as a split-screen, as in Figure 2-12. In this example, the text exceeds one page but only by a little. A scroll bar on the text side lets you scroll down to see the entire item.

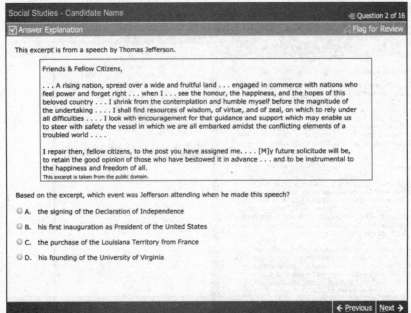

Figure 2-11:
An example of a Social Studies multiple-choice question.

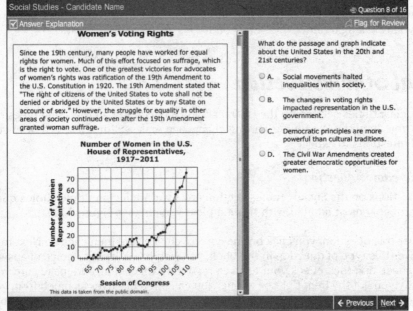

Figure 2-12:
A Social Studies multiple-choice question with a scroll bar.

Other types of Social Studies questions

The other questions on the Social Studies section of the test are just like the ones we discuss earlier in this chapter. They include questions with source text (the materials you need to read to answer the question) spread over several pages (as in Figure 2-13). The tabs on the top left of the screen indicate more pages of text. Each page is on a tab.

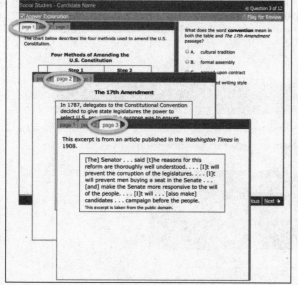

Figure 2-13:
An example of a multi-page Social Studies question with source text.

You'll also encounter fill-in-the-blank questions (as in Figure 2-14). On this type of item, you use the material presented in the passage to complete the box. As in other subject areas, you need a specific word or number for the blank. You must be accurate; spelling mistakes are scored as an error. In this book, you write the answer on the answer sheet.

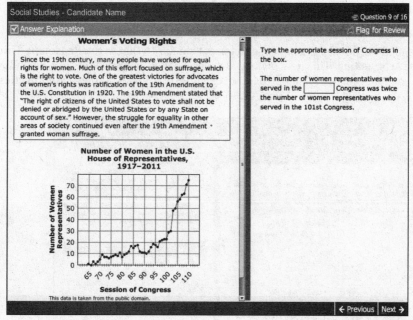

Figure 2-14:
A fill-in-the-blank example question.

Another type of problem is the drag and drop. You solve it the same way as the drag-and-drop problem on the Reasoning Through Language Arts section (refer to the earlier section "Drag-and-drop questions" for more information). Figure 2-15 is an example of a Social Studies drag-and-drop question.

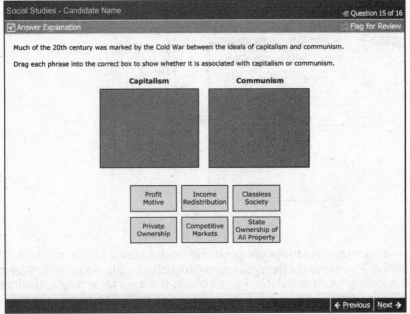

Figure 2-15: An example of a Social Studies drag-and-drop question.

The Extended Response

The Extended Response item also uses a format similar to that in the Reasoning Through Language Arts section. This item gives you several pages of source text and a window in which to write your answer. See Figure 2-16 for an example of a Social Studies Extended Response.

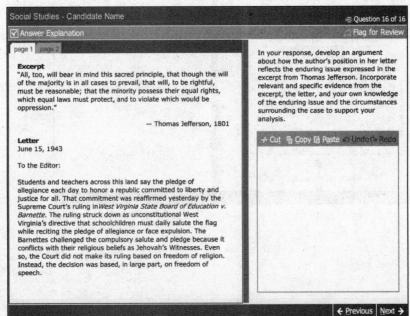

Figure 2-16: A sample Social Studies Extended Response.

In this book, you'll write your response on paper and ask one or two friends to grade it. If you're taking a GED test preparation course, the instructor may grade it for you. For information on the Social Studies section of the GED test, see Chapter 3.

Science section

When you take the Science section of the GED test, you have to answer a variety of the same types of questions in the other tests, all in 90 minutes. These sections focus on the slight differences you may see on the computer screen in the different types of questions.

Multiple-choice questions

Figure 2-17 shows an example of a multiple-choice Science question. Notice that the passage is longer than one page on the computer screen. Tabs on the side can move the text up and down. Moving it down reveals the other possible answers. Always be aware of the screen size limitation and advance pages or scroll up or down to ensure that you have all the information you need to make a decision.

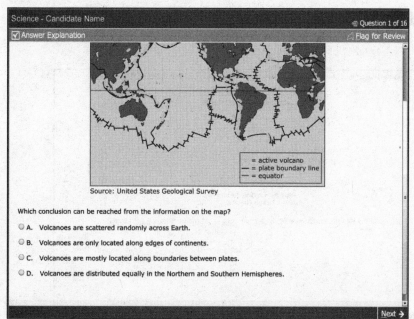

Figure 2-17: A sample Science multiple-choice question.

Copyright © 2014 GED Testing Service LLC

Fill-in-the-blank questions

Figure 2-18 shows an example of a fill-in-the-blank question. You see a statement or question followed by a box. You're expected to type the appropriate word(s) or number(s) into that box. In the example in Figure 2-18, the percent sign after each box indicates that you need to enter a number.

Drop-down menu questions

Questions involving a drop-down menu (see Figure 2-19) are similar to drop-down menu items in the other sections of the GED test. They're just a variation of the multiple-choice questions. You use the mouse to expand the choices and then again to select the correct one. (In the book, you mark your answer on the answer sheet.)

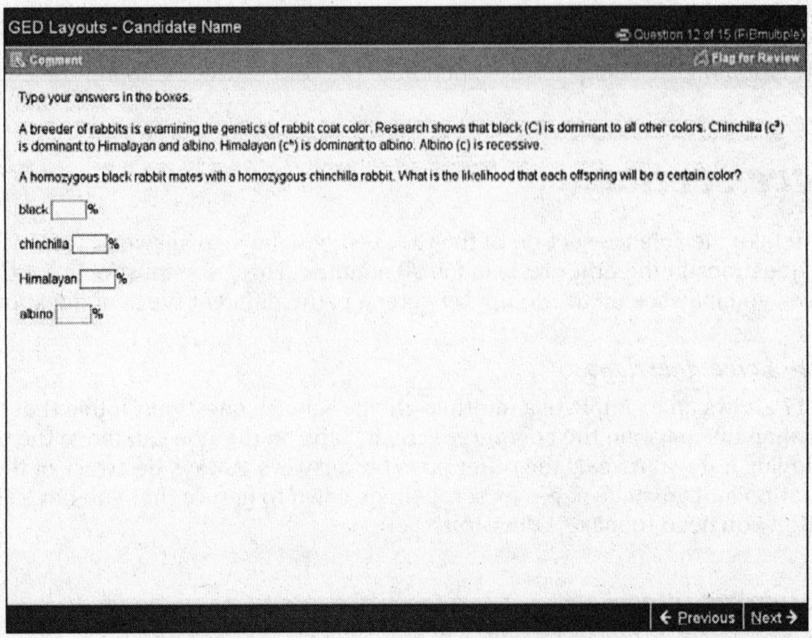

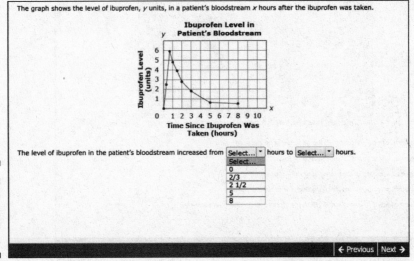

⌨ Comment ✎ Flag for Review

Type your answers in the boxes.

A breeder of rabbits is examining the genetics of rabbit coat color. Research shows that black (C) is dominant to all other colors. Chinchilla (c^3) is dominant to Himalayan and albino. Himalayan (c^h) is dominant to albino. Albino (c) is recessive.

A homozygous black rabbit mates with a homozygous chinchilla rabbit. What is the likelihood that each offspring will be a certain color?

black [   ] %

chinchilla [   ] %

Himalayan [   ] %

albino [   ] %

← Previous | Next →

Figure 2-18: A sample Science fill-in-the-blank question.

Copyright © 2014 GED Testing Service LLC

The graph shows the level of ibuprofen, *y* units, in a patient's bloodstream *x* hours after the ibuprofen was taken.

Ibuprofen Level in Patient's Bloodstream

The level of ibuprofen in the patient's bloodstream increased from [Select... ▼] hours to [Select... ▼] hours.

Select...
0
2/3
2 1/2
5
8

← Previous | Next →

Figure 2-19: An example of a drop-down menu question.

Copyright © 2014 GED Testing Service LLC

Drag-and-drop questions

The general format of these types of questions is similar throughout all the sections of the GED test (refer to Figures 2-4 and 2-15 for examples of this question type). On the computer, you'll see spaces and a list of possible answers to use in filling the spaces. Using the mouse, you can drag the word, numbers, or phrases to their appropriate location to create an answer. (In the book practice test sections, write the answers on the answer sheet provided. Always check your answers after completing each test section to make sure you understand the material.)

Hot-spot items

On the computer screen, hot spots are areas that, when clicked with a mouse, are recognized as correct answers. You can't tell where the areas are by looking at the screen; you have to figure it out and click on the spot that indicates the answer. Hot-spot formats appear in the Science and Mathematical Reasoning sections of the GED test. By clicking the mouse, you can draw a graph on the computer screen as in Figure 2-20.

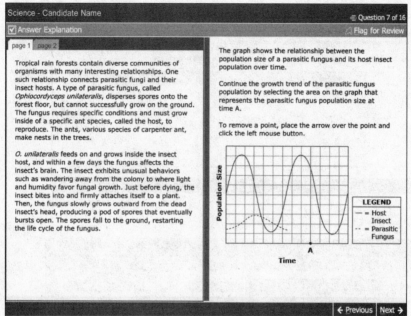

Figure 2-20: An example of a hot spot.

Short answer

This item requires more than just clicking on an answer choice. Like the Reasoning Through Language Arts and Social Studies Extended Response items, it's a written answer. The only difference is that in the Science section you have to write only a paragraph or two. You use the keyboard to type in the required information in the boxes. Figure 2-21 shows an example of a short-answer question on the computerized test.

Mathematical Reasoning section

The computerized GED test will look different on-screen than it does in this book. Here are some of the specific test formats you'll encounter in the Mathematical Reasoning section of the GED test.

Calculator

When you need a calculator, press the calculator tab, and a calculator appears that you can use to solve problems. See Figure 2-22. Find out more about the calculator on the GED test at www.gedtestingservice.com/educators/ticalc.

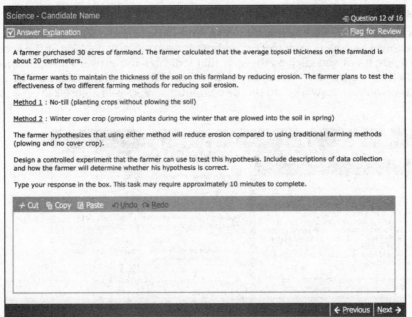

☑ Answer Explanation   ⚑ Flag for Review

A farmer purchased 30 acres of farmland. The farmer calculated that the average topsoil thickness on the farmland is about 20 centimeters.

The farmer wants to maintain the thickness of the soil on this farmland by reducing erosion. The farmer plans to test the effectiveness of two different farming methods for reducing soil erosion.

Method 1 : No-till (planting crops without plowing the soil)

Method 2 : Winter cover crop (growing plants during the winter that are plowed into the soil in spring)

The farmer hypothesizes that using either method will reduce erosion compared to using traditional farming methods (plowing and no cover crop).

Design a controlled experiment that the farmer can use to test this hypothesis. Include descriptions of data collection and how the farmer will determine whether his hypothesis is correct.

Type your response in the box. This task may require approximately 10 minutes to complete.

✂ Cut 📋 Copy 📋 Paste   ↺ Undo ↻ Redo

← Previous | Next →

Figure 2-21:
A sample short-answer question.

Copyright © 2014 GED Testing Service LLC

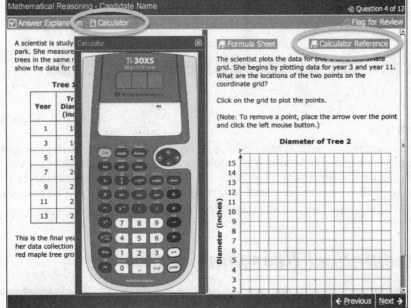

☑ Answer Explanation ⊟ Calculator   ⚑ Flag for Review

A scientist is study...
park. She measure...
trees in the same r...
show the data for t...

Tree 1...

Year	Tr... Diar... (in...
1	1...
3	1...
5	1...
7	2...
9	2...
11	2...
13	2...

This is the final yea...
her data collection...
red maple tree gro...

📄 Formula Sheet   📄 Calculator Reference

The scientist plots the data for tree 2 on a coordinate grid. She begins by plotting data for year 3 and year 11. What are the locations of the two points on the coordinate grid?

Click on the grid to plot the points.

(Note: To remove a point, place the arrow over the point and click the left mouse button.)

Diameter of Tree 2

← Previous | Next →

Figure 2-22:
The comput-erized GED test has a calculator that you can use on-screen.

Copyright © 2014 GED Testing Service LLC

Multiple-choice questions

Most of the items in the Mathematical Reasoning section are multiple-choice. The question presents you with four possible answer choices, only one of which is correct, although the other answer options may be close or incorporate common errors. Carefully read the item, question, and possible answers. Answer the question using the information provided in the item. The only exception is the list of formulas given when you click on the Formula button. Any of these can be used where appropriate. Figure 2-23 shows a basic example of a multiple-choice question.

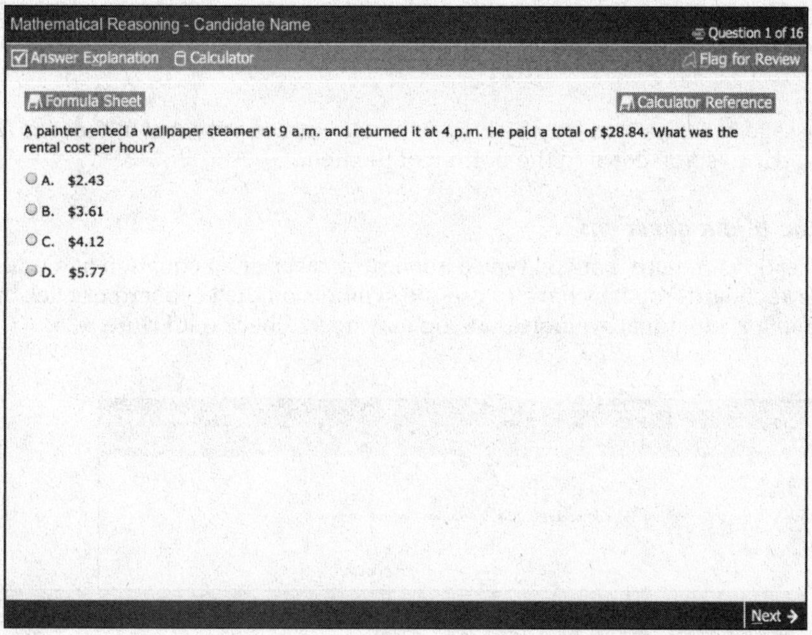

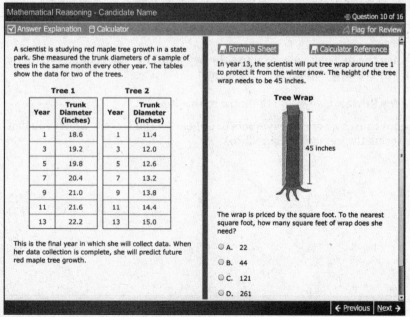

Figure 2-23:
An example
of a Math
multiple-
choice
question.

On the computer, you use the mouse to select the answer. (In the book's practice test section, you fill in the circle indicating the answer on an answer sheet. Always check your answer with the explanation.)

Sometimes multiple-choice questions appear in a split-screen with the question on the left-hand side and the possible answers on the right-hand side (see Figure 2-24). In either case, after you decide on the correct answer, you click the appropriate letter with your mouse. In the book, you have to mark your answer on the answer sheet.

Figure 2-24:
A split-
screen
multiple-
choice
question.

This particular question has some interesting buttons integrated into the format: a button to call up the calculator, one to fetch the formula sheet, and one for the calculator reference.

Some passages or questions may be longer than the space provided in the item. Look for the scroll bar to scroll down to the bottom of the item.

Fill-in-the-blank questions

These questions require that you type a numeric answer or an equation in a box provided, using the keyboard. You may have to use the symbols on the keyboard or click on the Symbol tab for additional symbols that you may need. Check out Figure 2-25.

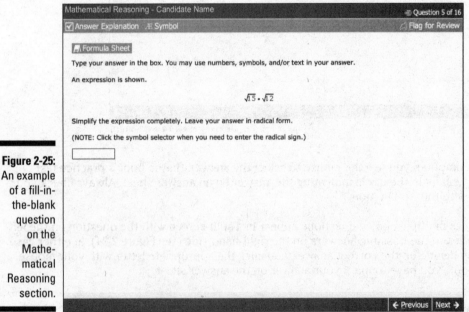

Figure 2-25: An example of a fill-in-the-blank question on the Mathematical Reasoning section.

After reading the item carefully, you use the keyboard to type your answer in the box. You'll notice two interesting additions in this format:

- ✔ **Flag for Review** allows you to return to this item.
- ✔ **Symbol** causes a series of symbols to appear on the screen, which you can use in answering the item (see Figure 2-26).

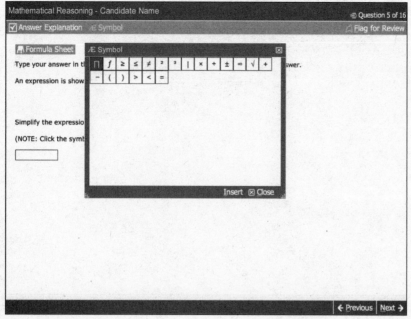

Figure 2-26:
An example
of the
Symbol box
popping up.

Other types of questions

In addition, the Mathematical Reasoning section has drop-down menu, drag-and-drop, and hot-spot questions just like the other three sections of the test. (Refer to those earlier sections for examples of what the questions look like on the computer screen.)

Chapter 3

Tackling the GED Test's Four Sections

*I*t's time to start your preparation for the GED test with a look at what to expect on the four sections that comprise the GED exam — Reasoning Through Language Arts, Social Studies, Science, and Mathematical Reasoning. You can take them all at once in one really long and tough day or individually whenever you feel sufficiently prepared. *Remember:* You don't have to do all the test sections on the same day. And after you pass a section, you're finished with that section forever. You'll earn your GED diploma whenever you've completed and passed all four test sections. In this chapter, we break down what you can expect on each section and help you prepare for answering the different question types. See Chapter 2 for examples of all the different questions and how they appear both on the computerized GED test and in the practice test sections in this book.

Working through the Reasoning Through Language Arts Section

We break the Reasoning Through Language Arts (RLA) section into two parts for easier study. One part deals with reading skills; the other deals with writing. On the actual RLA test section, these two skill sets are combined into one.

In this section, we offer some example questions for each part of the RLA section, which show you how the questions work and what's expected of you to answer them. You first answer a series of short items, mainly multiple-choice. However, you'll also see items in the form of fill-in-the-blanks, drag-and-drop, and drop-down menus. In each case, you need to look for the answer in the text presented to you. To find the answer, you may simply have to refer to the text, or you may have to draw conclusions from what you've read. And, finally, in the writing portion, you have sentence correction and the Extended Response, or essay.

The reading section

On this part of the RLA test section, you're given text to read, followed by a set of questions about that text, which tests your ability to read and comprehend. Some items will simply ask about content; other items will require analysis. The information you need to answer will be right in the text you read. Some items will ask you to draw conclusions based on the information in the text, which are the "why" or "how do you know" questions.

Here are two bits of collective wisdom: First, before taking the RLA section, read, read, and read some more. And, secondly, when taking the RLA section, read carefully; the answer is in the text. The best guarantee that you'll do well on this section is to become a fluent and analytical reader. Read editorials, analyze how the writers make their point, and provide supportive evidence of their points. Read newspaper stories to extract the bare-bones key points that make the story. Read and think about how the writer creates a mood, image, or point of view. Although you don't have to master any specific content before taking the reading portion of the RLA section, the more you read, the better-equipped you'll be to deal with this.

We go into detail about the types of questions to expect on the RLA section and how to answer them in the following sections.

Multiple-choice questions

Most of the items on the Reasoning Through Language Arts section are some form of a multiple-choice problem, where you choose from four answers. (Refer to Chapter 2 for how multiple-choice questions appear in this section on the computer screen when you're taking the actual GED test.)

Multiple-choice items give you the correct answer but make it harder by adding three wrong answers. So when you see this item on the GED test, read the question first and then the text, looking for related material. Go back to the answer choices and eliminate the obviously wrong ones as you progress. Eventually, you'll be left with one or two choices from which to pick your answer.

Pick the most correct, most complete answer from the choices offered. You may find, based on your previous knowledge, that none of the choices is complete. However, you need to go with the materials in the text, so use the answer choice closest to what is in the text.

The best advice for completing the reading portion of the RLA section is

(A) Read, read, and read some more.

(B) Memorize every poem ever written by Shakespeare.

(C) Read the short versions of any famous books you can find.

(D) None of the above.

The correct answer is Choice (A). You don't have to know any specific content for this section of the test, but you need to be able to read quickly and accurately and understand what you've read. The only way to do that is to practice and practice and practice some more.

Here are a couple of examples of multiple-choice questions like you'll see on the GED test.

People have a natural metabolic "set point" that is predetermined at birth and influences just how slim or heavy they will be. That is why it is difficult for the obese to lose weight beyond a particular point and for the slim to gain and retain weight for long. Some studies now suggest that the chemicals in clothing and upholstery flame-retardants interfere with that set point when they are absorbed into the body. This may affect a child in the womb and even after birth, which is one reason some jurisdictions are banning flame-retardants from children's clothing. California is even considering banning them from upholstery, another common application.

Why are chemicals in upholstery potentially harmful?

(A) They can cause retardation.

(B) They interfere with the natural metabolic set point.

(C) California is considering banning them.

(D) None of the above

The correct answer is Choice (B), which is clearly stated in the text. Choice (A) may be true, but it isn't supported by the text, so if you went with that choice, you probably mis-read the text. Choices (C) and (D) are irrelevant or wrong. Other reasons to place a ban on flame-retardants should be considered, but you're not asked about them, so stick with the options offered.

Why is anyone concerned about the metabolic set point?

(A) The set point determines how much people will weigh. Anything that interferes with that is dangerous.

(B) Most people want to be slim.

(C) People don't want chemicals in their bodies.

(D) People are against the misuse of chemicals in the environment.

The correct answer is Choice (A). The text states that these chemicals interfere with the set point, and that is dangerous, causing obesity or drastic underweight. Choices (B), (C), and (D) are all possibly true but aren't supported by the text.

Drag-and-drop questions

The Reasoning Through Language Arts section also uses the drag-and-drop question type. This item requires you to drag and drop information from one location on the screen to another. Usually, the purpose is for you to reorder something from least important to most, to place events into a sequence, or simply to select a series of items or choices that apply to the question. For example, you may be asked to pick two or three words that describe a person or event in the text, from a choice of four or five options. Doing so is relatively simple: You just click on the item to move with your mouse, and then, while holding down the mouse button, you drag the item to the new location. When you reach the new location, let go of the mouse button, and drop the item. If you've moved it properly, it will stay where you dropped it. Check out Chapter 2 to see how a drag-and-drop question looks on the computerized GED test.

To prepare for the drag-and-drop items on the GED test, practice critical reading. When you're reading editorials and articles, try to pull out key points and look for biases or unsupported conclusions.

Answering a drag-and-drop item requires you to

(A) Do some heavy lifting.

(B) Type directions into a box.

(C) Click on and move a choice of an answer.

(D) Play a lot of Solitaire.

Choice (C) is correct. Choice (A) refers more to a job in the real world and not taking a test. Choice (B) applies to the directions for fill-in-the-blank or Extended Response items. Choice (D) is one way to waste time that could be better spent preparing for the test.

Here are a couple types of drag-and-drop problems that you may encounter on the GED test.

> Bradley was determined to get the job. Although he wanted to go to the movies with Keesha, he also needed to work, and the job interview looked promising. He loved his job at the mill, but it was not enough to provide him with the income he needed. Of course, the hours were great, but the hourly rate was not. He could have left early, gone to the interview, and still had his date with Keesha, but that would have created problems with his boss at the mill. Bradley made the only choice he could. He finished his day at the mill and then went to the job interview. Keesha waited by the phone but never heard from him.

Put the names and phrases in order of importance to Bradley, with the most important on top and the least at the bottom.

(A) Keesha

(B) job at the mill

(C) job interview

(D) a raise

Based on the text, the best order is Choice (D), *a raise;* Choice (C), *job interview;* Choice (B), *job at the mill;* and then Choice (A), *Keesha.*

Which one of these terms best applies to Bradley? Indicate your answer in the box on the right.

(A) friendly

(B) good boyfriend

(C) hardworking

(D) determined

The correct answer is *determined.* The text states that "Bradley was determined to get the job." He left his girlfriend in the lurch, not even leaving his regular work early to date Keesha, so he is certainly not the best of boyfriends. He may be friendly and hardworking, but the overwhelming point is determination.

In the practice Reasoning Through Language Arts test section in Chapter 5, when you see an item in this format, you see the content of the boxes as words or phrases preceded by capital letters. You can then enter the letters into boxes on the answer sheet to indicate your choices.

Fill-in-the-blank questions

You're likely familiar with the fill-in-the-blank question type. It requires you to find one word or number in the source text that answers a question and then type (or write) that word or number in a space. On the GED test, the blank that you need to fill in looks like an empty box. Just click in that box and type in your answer. For the fill-in-the-blank items in this book, you can write your answer directly in the box or on the answer sheet for the practice test sections. Refer to the source text in the previous section to answer this question.

Bradley's girlfriend is named ⬚⬚⬚⬚⬚.

There is nothing fancy about fill-in-the-blank items; they simply require good reading skills.

The writing section

The writing part of the Reasoning Through Language Arts section evaluates your ability to use correct spelling and grammar to write clearly and succinctly. It tests your ability in various ways. Some questions ask you to select the correct alternative to a misspelled or grammatically incorrect sentence. Others ask you to provide a better wording for a sentence or select the best choice of words for some text. The text will vary from business letters to extracts from novels. They can be based on instruction manuals for an MP3 player, a newspaper story, or a contract.

To study and prepare for these types of questions, try the following tips:

✔ Review your spelling and grammar skills.

✔ Use the local library to find high-school grammar texts or look for free grammar and spelling quizzes online. Some online quizzes will correct your answers immediately, giving you excellent feedback on what you know and what needs improvement.

✔ After you take the practice test section in Chapter 5, you may see some areas where you need to improve, so you can review those areas, using *English Grammar For Dummies,* 2nd Edition, by Geraldine Woods (Wiley), or other grammar books. As you work on your grammar and writing skills, periodically redo the practice test section to see how much you have improved.

Question types

Most of the questions in the writing section are multiple-choice items, but you'll also see some fill-in-the-blanks and drag-and-drop items (see "The reading section" for an overview of these question types). This section includes one other question type: the drop-down menu. In these questions, you select the correct alternative from a number of choices. Like multiple-choice, the drop-down menu will usually include four options (sometimes you'll see as few as three).

The drop-down menu items consist of a sentence with a box on the line containing a down arrow and the word *select*. When you click on Select, several alternative word or sentence choices appear. You click on the best choice, and the sentence appears with your selection. *Note:* In this book, you won't see a drop-down menu but just a list of answer choices. See Chapter 2 for details on this question format.

When we got there, we discovered _____ car was missing.

(A) their

(B) they're

(C) there

The correct answer is Choice (A), *their*. These words are *homonyms* — words that sound alike but have different meanings. Choice (A), *their,* shows possession, as in "their book"; Choice (B), *they're* is a contraction of *they are;* and Choice (C), *there,* is a location in space or time.

Dear Mr. Jones

(1) We would like to thank you for you're kind words. (2) As a manufacturer, we try to produce the best possible goods for consumers. (3) The keyboard's we produce do not often receive the recognition your review gives us, and it is much appreciated.

Sentence 1: **We would like to thank you for you're kind words.**

What changes should be made to Sentence 1?

(A) change *would* to *wood*

(B) capitalize *thank you*

(C) change *you're* to *your*

(D) all of the above

The correct answer is Choice (C). It refers to the misuse of *you're,* a contraction of *you are,* when *your,* as in ownership or possession, is appropriate. Choice (A) is another example of homonyms, but the correct word, *would,* is used in the sentence so no change needed there. Choice (C) is wrong in suggesting a capitalization in the middle of the sentence.

Sentence 2: **As a manufacturer, we try to produce the best possible goods for consumers.**

What corrections need to be made in Sentence 2?

(A) change *manufacturer* to *manufactures*

(B) change *produce* to *produse*

(C) delete the comma after *manufacturer*

(D) none of the above

In this case, the answer is Choice (D), *none of the above*. No error occurs in the sentence. Although often the *all of the above* or *none of the above* answer choices are thrown in to fool you, don't fall into the trap of ignoring the option. Sometimes it does apply.

Sentence 3: **The keyboard's we produce do not often receive the recognition your review gives us, and it is much appreciated.**

What changes need to be made in Sentence 3?

(A) change *keyboard's* to *keyboards*

(B) change *receive* to *recieve*

(C) change *appreciated* to *appreciation*

(D) capitalize *keyboard's*

The correct answer is Choice (A). When you present the plural of *keyboard,* it's *keyboards,* without the apostrophe. Choice (B) is an attempt to lead you into error: The spelling change suggests that you use *recieve,* a common spelling error.

The other questions will be the same as for the reading section. The big difference for this section is that you can study for this section by checking out lists of commonly misspelled words, reviewing grammar and punctuation rules, and getting familiar with homonyms and their proper use.

The Extended Response

When you finish the first part of the Reasoning Through Language Arts (RLA) section, including all the question types we discuss earlier, you start on the Extended Response — where you write an essay by analyzing arguments presented in two pieces of sample text. You get 45 minutes to work through this part of the RLA section, and you can't tack on extra time from the previous section. So if you find that you have time left on the first part, go back and review some of the questions where you had difficulties before starting the Extended Response. And remember, after the Extended Response, you have a 10 minute break and then another hour of more multiple-choice type items.

For the Extended Response item, you must write a proper essay, with a clear thesis statement, a proper introduction, followed by four or six paragraphs of supporting argument, and a concluding paragraph. You'll have an erasable tablet on which to make rough notes, and if you need more, you can get additional tablets. You won't use or have access to paper, pencils, or dictionaries. When you complete your rough draft of your essay, you write it into a window on the computer that functions like a word processor. The word processor is basic and doesn't have a grammar- or spell-checker. You're expected to know how to write properly.

The topic you're given to write on is based on given source material, usually consisting of two documents with different or opposing opinions. You're expected to analyze the source material and write an appropriate analytical response. You must show that you can read and understand the source material, do a critical analysis, and prepare a reasoned response based on materials drawn from that source text.

In your essay, you analyze both positions and then give your opinion or explain your viewpoint. Remember to back up your points with specific facts from the source material. When you write this essay, make sure it's a series of interconnected paragraphs on a single topic. Not only should the entire essay begin with an introduction and end with a conclusion, but also each paragraph needs an introductory sentence and a concluding sentence.

Write only on the assigned topic. To make sure you understand what the topic is about, read it several times. Essays written off topic don't receive scores. If you don't get sufficient points on the Extended Response, you likely won't pass the other portion of the RLA section, either.

Your essay is evaluated on the following points:

- ✔ Your argument is based specifically on the given source material.

- ✔ You correctly use the evidence from the source material to support your argument.

- ✔ You use valid arguments and separate the supported claims in the material from the unsupported or false claims either in the material or your head.

- ✔ Your flow of ideas is logical and well organized.

- ✔ You correctly and appropriately use style, structure, vocabulary, and grammar.

Consider this example of an Extended Response item:

"I will give up my muscle car when the world runs out of oil, not before. . . ."

"We need to find alternatives to gasoline-powered vehicles. Climate change is a real threat, and burning fossil fuels contributes to that problem. . . ."

These two opinions are the beginnings of an editorial, taking obviously different positions.

In this example, you start by determining which argument you see as stronger. Then, you make a list of information that may go into your essay to back up your argument. Trim out any information that doesn't pertain to the topic. Use unsubstantiated opinions as part of your evidence that one side or the other has a weak case.

When you start writing your essay, start with a good, strong introductory sentence that will catch a reader's attention. When you're satisfied with your introductory sentence, review your list of information. Follow that introductory sentence with a couple of sentences outlining, without explanation, your key points. Now turn each key point into a paragraph, paying attention to the flow between paragraphs to show that one relates to the previous one. When you have all these paragraphs, it's time for a conclusion. The easiest way to write a good conclusion is to restate your evidence briefly and state that this indeed proves your point. Don't just rewrite your information, but summarize it in a memorable way. This may be difficult the first time, but with practice, it can become second nature.

If you have time, you can test how well your essay works and stays on topic. Read the introduction, the first sentence of every paragraph, and then the conclusion. They should all have the same basic points and flow together nicely. If something seems out of place, you need to go back and review.

To prepare for this part of the test, in a few months leading up to your test date, read newspapers and news magazines. Analyze how arguments are presented and how the writers try to form and sway your opinion. Examine how well they present their data and how they use relevant and irrelevant data to persuade the reader. Doing so can give you practice in critical reading and in developing your opinions and viewpoints based on others' writings.

Handling the Social Studies Section

For the Social Studies section, you have to answer a variety of items. You have 90 minutes to answer the questions, multiple-choice items, other short items, and one Extended Response (essay). You should leave yourself 25 minutes for the Extended Response, but in this section (unlike the Reasoning Through Language Arts, RLA, section), your time is one block, and you can allocate it any way you like. The short items use the same format as the RLA section items: multiple-choice questions, fill-in-the-blanks, and drag-and-drop items (see the earlier sections on Reasoning Through Language Arts for details). These questions deal with the following subject areas:

- Civics and government (50 percent)
- American history (20 percent)
- Economics (15 percent)
- Geography and the world (15 percent)

The items in this section are based on written texts (source texts), pictures, charts, tables, graphs, photographs, political cartoons, diagrams, or maps. These textual and pictorial excerpts come from a variety of sources, such as government documents, academic texts, material from work-related documents, and atlases.

You can do only a limited amount of studying for this section. The information to answer each item is in the text or graphic that comes with the question. You need to analyze the material and draw conclusions based on what's presented. However, you can prepare by reading some books that offer you a basic outline of American history and learn about how government functions. Read the newspapers to follow current events and the business section of your newspaper for economics. You don't need to go into great depth or memorize pages of dates and names, but you should have an idea of the general flow of history. You also need to know how your governments — from federal to local — work.

A second skill you need to master for this test section is reading and extracting information from maps, charts, and tables. On the Social Studies section, you'll see a map with different shadings and will have to determine what the shadings mean and what the difference is between a light gray area on the map and the dark gray. They're not just decoration. If you look carefully at all the text and boxes with information on the map or chart, you'll see that everything has a meaning. So get an atlas, and practice reading maps.

The other types of questions and the Extended Response on the Social Studies section of the test are just like the items that we discuss in the Reasoning Through Language Arts section in this chapter and in Chapter 2. The only difference on the Extended Response is that you can write a shorter essay, but then you also have less time to do so. However, in the Social Studies Extended Response, some general knowledge of American history is expected.

You may see the following types of problems on the Social Studies section.

The following question is based on this table.

Type of Religion	Date Started (Approximate)	Sacred Texts
Buddhism	500 BC	None
Christianity	33 AD	Bible (Old Testament and New Testament)
Hinduism	4000 BC	Vedas; Upanishads
Islam	600 AD	Qur'an; Hadith
Judaism	2000 BC	Hebrew Bible; Talmud

According to the table, Hinduism

(A) started in 600 AD

(B) uses the Qur'an as one of its sacred texts

(C) is the oldest religion

(D) has no known sacred texts

The correct answer is Choice (C). The table shows that Hinduism is the oldest of the five religions listed because it began in 4000 BC.

The following question is based on this excerpt from the diary of Christopher Columbus.

Monday, 6 August. The rudder of the caravel Pinta became loose, being broken or unshipped. It was believed that this happened by the contrivance of Gomez Rascon and Christopher Quintero, who were on board the caravel, because they disliked the voyage. The Admiral says he had found them in an unfavorable disposition before setting out. He was in much anxiety at not being able to afford any assistance in this case, but says that it somewhat quieted his apprehensions to know that Martin Alonzo Pinzon, Captain of the Pinta, was a man of courage and capacity. Made progress, day and night, of twenty-nine leagues.

Why would Rascon and Quintero have loosened the rudder?

(A) They were trying to repair the rudder.

(B) The Admiral found them in an unfavorable disposition.

(C) The captain was very competent.

(D) They did not want to be on the voyage.

The correct answer is Choice (D). This answer is the only one supported by the text. The others may be related to statements in the passage, but they don't answer the question.

The following question is based on this graph.

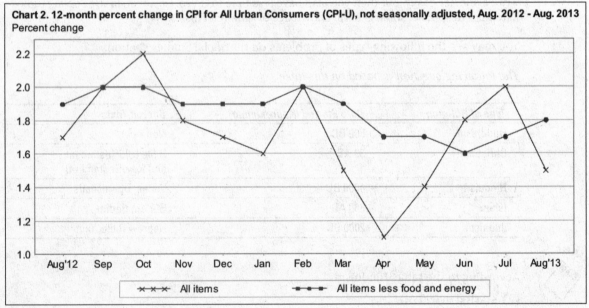

Chart 2. 12-month percent change in CPI for All Urban Consumers (CPI-U), not seasonally adjusted, Aug. 2012 - Aug. 2013

Illustration courtesy of the United States Department of Labor

What effect do energy and food prices have on inflation?

(A) They level out the range of change over time.

(B) They magnify the range of change over time.

(C) They increase the rate of inflation.

(D) They have no effect.

The correct answer is Choice (B). The inclusion of food and energy prices makes the graph values swing much wider. The combined graph line shows much wider variation. Hence, food and energy prices magnify inflation.

The following question asks you to fill in the blank based on the previous graph.

The range of inflation for "all items" shown on the graph is [＿＿＿＿]%.

The correct answer is 1.1. The highest value for inflation on the "all items" line is 2.2% for October. The lowest value, in April, is about 1.1%. Therefore, the range is approximately 1.1%.

Knowing How to Grapple the Science Section

When you take the Science section of the GED test, you have to answer the same variety of question formats, including multiple-choice, fill-in-the-blank, drop-down menu, drag and drop, hot spot, and short answer, all in 80 minutes. The questions deal with the following topics:

- Life science (40 percent)
- Physical science, including chemistry and physics (40 percent)
- Earth and space science (20 percent)

Most of the information you need to answer the items on the Science section is given to you in the passages and other excerpts, although to get a perfect score, you're expected to have picked up a basic knowledge of science. However, even if you correctly answer only the questions based entirely on the information presented, you should get a score high enough to pass.

Although you won't be expected to be an expert on the various topics in the Science section, you will be expected to understand the words. To accomplish this, read as widely as you can in Science books. If you run across words you don't understand, write them down with a definition or explanation. Doing so will provide a vocabulary list for you to review before the test.

You must read and understand the passages in the Science section to be able to select the best choice for an answer. Practice reading quickly and accurately. Because you have a time limit, practice skimming passages to look for key words. The less time you spend on the passages, the more time you'll have to answer the item, and the more time you'll have at the end of the test to review your answers and attempt questions that you found difficult the first time you read them. Attempt to answer every question. You may get a mark for your answer if you try it but you can't get a mark for an item you've left out.

The Science section also includes short-answer questions in which you respond to a passage or passages in a coherent logical way. ***Remember:*** You're expected to write a response that might be expected of someone ready for employment or college, not a public school student or someone preparing for a doctoral thesis. You should be able to include material from the passage and some from your general knowledge. Because the simplified word processor on the test has limitations, check your spelling and grammar carefully. In science, make sure that if you use a word from your reading, it's spelled correctly and used correctly. Above all, don't panic. If you've prepared, you'll do fine. See Chapter 2 for an example short-answer item.

Here are some sample problems similar to those that may be in the Science section on the GED test.

The following questions are based on this excerpt from a press release.

> A key feature of the Delta 4's operation is the use of a common booster core, or CBC, a rocket stage that measures some 150 feet long and 16 feet wide. By combining one or more CBCs with various upper stages or strap-on solid rocket boosters, the Delta 4 can handle an extreme range of satellite applications for military, civilian, and commercial customers.

The CBC in this context is a

(A) Canadian Broadcasting Corporation

(B) common booster core

(C) cooperative boosters corps

(D) common ballistic cavalier

The correct answer is Choice (B). After all, it's the only answer choice mentioned in the passage. Skimming the passage would give you an idea of where to look for a fuller explanation of the abbreviation.

How can the Delta 4 handle a wide range of applications?

(A) developing a Delta 5

(B) continuing research

(C) using the CBC as the base of a rocket ship

(D) creating a common core booster

The correct answer is Choice (C). The passage says that "By combining one or more CBCs with various upper stages or strap-on solid rocket boosters . . . ," so Choice (C) comes closest to answering the question.

Conquering the Mathematical Reasoning Section

The Mathematical Reasoning section of the GED test covers the following four major areas:

- Algebra, equations, and patterns
- Data analysis, statistics, and probability
- Measurement and geometry
- Number operations

More specifically, about 45 percent of the questions focus on quantitative problem solving and the other about 55 percent focuses on algebraic problem solving.

The Mathematical Reasoning section has many of the same types of problems as the other sections (multiple-choice, fill-in-the-blank, and so on). Check out Chapter 2 for how these questions look on the computerized test.

Mathematics is mathematics. That may sound simple, but it isn't. To succeed on the Mathematical Reasoning section, you should have a good grasp of the basic operations: addition, subtraction, multiplication, and division. You should be able to perform these operations quickly and accurately and, in the case of simple numbers, perform them mentally. The more automatic and accurate your responses are, the less time you'll need for each item, and the greater your chances are of finishing the test on time with a few minutes to spare to check any items you may have skipped or answers you want to double-check.

The other skill you should try to master is reading quickly and accurately. The items are written in English prose and you're expected to know how to answer the item from the passage presented. Try to increase your reading speed and test yourself for accuracy. If you are a slow reader, search "speed reading" on any search engine to get some hints. You can check for accuracy by writing down what you think you read without looking at the passage and seeing how close you can come to it. More important than knowing whether you can recall each and every word is knowing how accurate you are so that you can compensate for issues before the test.

Consider the following items (one traditional multiple-choice question and two questions that use different formats that you'll encounter on the computer) that are similar to what you may see on the Mathematical Reasoning section.

A right-angle triangle has a hypotenuse of 5 feet and one side that is 36 inches long. What is the length of the other side in feet?

(A) 3 ft

(B) 48 ft

(C) 6 ft

(D) 4 ft

The correct answer is Choice (D). Using the Pythagorean theorem (a formula that's given to you on the formula page of the test), you know that $a^2 + b^2 = c^2$, where c is the hypotenuse and a and b are either of the other two sides. Because you know the hypotenuse and one side, turn the equation around so that it reads $a^2 = c^2 - b^2$.

You can recall the page of formulas on the computer when needed. Remember that the fewer times you need to call it up, the more time you'll have to answer questions.

To get c^2, you square the hypotenuse: $(5)(5) = 25$.

The other side is given in inches — to convert inches to feet, divide by 12: $36/12 = 3$. To get b^2, square this side: $(3)(3) = 9$.

Now solve the equation for a: $a^2 = 25 - 9$ or $a^2 = 16$. Take the square root of both sides, and you get $a = 4$.

The Mathematical Reasoning section presents real-life situations in the items. So if you find yourself answering 37 feet to a question about the height of a room or $3.00 for an annual salary, recheck your answer because you're probably wrong.

The following question asks you to fill in the blank.

Barb is counting the number of boxes in a warehouse. In the first storage area, she finds 24 boxes. The second area contains 30 boxes. The third area contains 28 boxes. If the warehouse has 6 storage areas where it stores boxes, and the areas have an average of 28 boxes, the total number of boxes in the last three areas is ⬚.

The correct answer is 86. If the warehouse has 6 storage areas and it has an average of 28 boxes in each, it has (6)(28) = 168 boxes in the warehouse. The first three areas have 24 + 30 + 28 = 82 boxes in them. The last three areas must have 168 – 82 = 86 boxes in them.

A rectangle has one corner on the origin. The base goes from the origin to the point (3, 0). The right side goes from (3, 0) to (3, 4). Place the missing point on the graph.

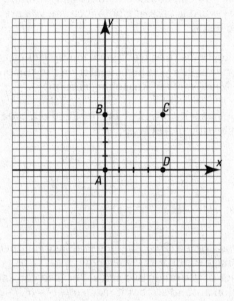

The correct answer is to put point B at (0, 4). Because you're using a book and not a computer, you just write your answer on the answer sheet. If you shade the three points given on the graph, you see that a fourth point at (0, 4) creates the rectangle. Draw the point as shown on the graph.

Chapter 4

Succeeding on the GED Test

- -

In This Chapter

▶ Getting ready in the weeks and the night before and the day of the test

▶ Relying on practice tests

▶ Figuring out what to expect on test day

▶ Nailing down important test-taking strategies

▶ Staying calm and relaxed while you take the test

- -

You may never have taken a standardized test before. Or if you have, you may wake up sweating in the middle of the night from nightmares about your past experiences. Whether you've experienced the joys or sorrows of standardized tests, to succeed on the GED test, you must know how to perform well on this type of test, which consists mostly of multiple-choice questions.

The good news is, you've come to the right spot to find out more about this type of test. This chapter explains some important pointers on how to prepare on the days and nights before the test, what to do on the morning of the test, and what to do during the test to be successful. You also discover some important test-taking strategies to help you feel confident.

Leading Up to Test Time

Doing well on the GED test involves more than walking into the test site and answering the questions. You need to be prepared for the challenges in the tests. To ensure that you're ready to tackle the test head-on, make sure you do the following leading up to the test:

✔ **Get enough sleep.** We're sorry if we sound like your parents, but it's true — you shouldn't take tests when you're approaching exhaustion. Plan your time so you can get a good night's sleep for several days before the test and avoid excess caffeine. If you prepare ahead of time, you'll be ready and sleep will come easier.

✔ **Eat a good breakfast.** A healthy breakfast fuels your mind and body. You have to spend several hours taking the test, and you definitely don't want to falter during that time. Eat some protein, such as eggs, bacon, or sausage with toast for breakfast. Avoid sugars (donuts, jelly, fruit) because they can cause you to tire easily. You don't want your empty stomach fighting with your full brain.

✔ **Take some deep breaths.** During your trip to the testing site, prepare yourself mentally for the test. Clear your head of all distractions, practice deep breathing, and imagine yourself acing the test. Don't panic.

✔ **Start at the beginning, not the end.** Remember that the day of the test is the end of a long journey of preparation and not the beginning. It takes time to build mental muscles.

✔ **Be on time.** Make sure you know what time the test begins and the exact location of your test site. Arrive early. If necessary, take a practice run to make sure you have enough time to get from your home or workplace to the testing center. You don't need the added pressure of worrying about whether you can make it to the test on time. In fact, this added pressure can create industrial-strength panic in the calmest of people.

Traffic happens. No one can plan for it, but you can leave extra time to make sure it doesn't ruin your day. Plan your route and practice it. Then leave extra time in case a meteor crashes into the street and the crowd that gathers around it stalls your progress. Even though the GED test is now administered on a computer and it's not necessary for everyone to start at the same time, test centers are open only for certain hours, and if they close before you finish, you won't get any sympathy. Check the times the test center is open. Examiners won't show you a lot of consideration if you show up too late to complete the test or tests because you didn't check the times. They have even less sympathy if you show up on the wrong date.

Using Practice Tests to Your Advantage

Taking practice GED tests is important for a few reasons, including the following:

✔ **They give you an indication of how well you know the material.** One or two tests won't give you a definite answer, because you need to do four or five tests to cover all possible topics, but they do give you an indication of where you stand.

✔ **They confirm whether you know how to use the computer to answer the questions.** Until you try, you simply won't know for sure.

✔ **They familiarize you with the test format.** You can read about test questions, but you can't actually understand them until you have worked through several.

✔ **They can ease your stress.** A successful run-through on a practice test allows you to feel more comfortable and confident in your own abilities to take the GED test successfully and alleviate your overall anxiety.

You can find a practice test of each section in Chapters 5 through 8. The practice tests are an important part of any preparation program. They're the feedback mechanism that you may normally get from a private tutor. As long as you check your answers after the practice test and read the answer explanations in Chapter 9, you can benefit from taking practice tests. If possible, take as many practice tests as you can before taking the actual GED test. You can find more practice tests at www.gedtestingservice.com/educators/freepracticetest and a few more sample questions at www.gedtestingservice.com/testers/sample-questions. Use a search engine to find more examples of practice tests online.

Finding Out What to Take to the GED Test

The GED test may be the most important exam you ever take. Treat it seriously and come prepared. Make sure you bring the following items with you on test day:

✔ **You:** The most important thing to bring to the GED test is obviously you. If you enroll to take the tests, you have to show up; otherwise, you'll receive a big fat zero and lose your testing fee. If something unfortunate happens after you enroll, contact the test center and explain your situation to the test administrators. They may reschedule the test without an additional charge.

✔ **Correct identification:** Before test officials let you into the room to take the test, they want to make sure you're you. Bring the approved photo ID — your state GED office can tell you what's an approved form of photo ID. Have your ID in a place where you can reach it easily. And when asked to identify yourself, don't pull out a mirror and say, "Yep, that's me."

✔ **Fees you still owe:** The same people don't run all test centers. With some, you may have to pay in advance, when booking the test. If so, bring your receipt to avoid any misunderstandings. Others may allow you to pay at the door. If so, find out whether you can use cash, check, or credit card. The amount of the GED test registration fee also varies from state to state. (Check with your local administrator to confirm when and where the fee has to be paid and how to pay it.) If you don't pay the fee, you can't take the exam.

If needed, you may be able to get financial assistance to help with the testing fees. Further, if you do the tests one section at a time, which we recommend, you can probably pay for each test section as you complete it. Check with your state or local education authorities.

✔ **Registration confirmation:** The registration confirmation is your proof that you did register. If you're taking the tests in an area where everybody knows you and everything you do, you may not need the confirmation, but we still suggest you take it anyway. It's light and doesn't take up much room in your pocket.

✔ **Other miscellaneous items:** In the instructions you receive after you register for the test, you get a list of what you need to bring with you. Besides yourself and the items we list previously, other items you want to bring or wear include the following:

- **Comfortable clothes and shoes:** When you're taking the test, you want to be as relaxed as possible. Uncomfortable clothes and shoes may distract you from doing your best. You're taking the GED test, not modeling the most recent couture.

- **A bottle of water or some coffee:** Check with the administrators whether drinks are allowed beforehand. Computers and liquids don't mix, so they may not allow you to take drinks in with you. Mints and gum may be an alternative.

- **Reading glasses:** If you need glasses to read a computer monitor, don't forget to bring them to the test. Bring a spare pair, if you have one. You can't do the test if you can't read the screen.

The rules about what enters the testing room are strict. Don't take any chances. If an item isn't on the list of acceptable items and isn't normal clothing, leave it at home. The last place on earth to discuss whether you can bring something into the test room is at the door on test day. If you have questions, contact the test center in advance. Check out www. GEDcomputer.com to start the registration process and find a list of sites close to your home with their addresses and phone numbers. You can also call 800-62-MYGED to ask your questions of real people.

Whatever you do, be sure not to bring the following with you to the GED testing center:

✔ Books

✔ Calculator (one is provided for you on-screen — see Chapter 2)

✔ Notes or scratch paper

✔ MP3 players or tablets

✔ Cellphone (leave it at home or in your car)

✔ Anything valuable, like a laptop computer, that you don't feel comfortable leaving outside the room while you take the test

Making Sure You're Comfortable before the Test Begins

You usually take the GED test in an examination room with at least one official (sometimes called a *proctor* or *examiner*) who's in charge of the test. (Some locations have smaller test centers that have space for no more than 15 test-takers at a time.) In either case, the test is the same.

As soon as you sit down to take the GED test, take a few moments before the test actually starts to relax and get comfortable. You're going to be in the chair for quite some time, so bunker down. Keep these few tips in mind before you begin:

- **Make sure that the screen is at a comfortable height and adjust your chair to a height that suits you.** Unlike a pen-and-paper test, you'll be working with a monitor and keyboard. Although you can shift the keyboard around and maybe change the angle of the monitor, generally you're stuck in that position for the duration of the test. If you need to make any adjustments, make them before you start. You want to feel as physically comfortable as possible.

- **Find out whether you can have something to drink at your computer station.** You may depend on a cup of coffee to keep you upright and thinking. Even a bottle of water may make your life easier. If your test center allows a drink, get one before you start so you can concentrate on the test.

- **Go to the bathroom before you start.** This may sound like a silly suggestion, but it all goes to being comfortable. You don't need distractions. Even if bathroom breaks are permitted during the test, you don't want to take away time from the test.

The proctor reads the test instructions to you and lets you log into the computer to start the test. Listen carefully to these instructions so you know how much time you have to take the test as well as any other important information. Only the Reasoning Through Language Arts test has a ten-minute break built into the time. The other tests are 90 minutes without a break. (Refer to the next section for how long each test lasts.)

Discovering Important Test-Taking Strategies

You can increase your score by mastering a few smart test-taking strategies. To help you do so, we give you some tips in these sections on how to

- Plan your time.
- Determine the question type.
- Figure out how to answer the different types of questions.
- Guess intelligently.
- Review your work.

Watching the clock: Using your time wisely

When you start the computerized version of the GED test, you may feel pressed for time and have the urge to rush through the questions. We strongly advise that you don't. You have sufficient time to do the test at a reasonable pace. You have only a certain amount of time for each section in the GED exam, so time management is an important part of succeeding on the test. You need to plan ahead and use your time wisely as you move through the test.

You must complete each section in one sitting, except for the Reasoning Through Language Arts test. There, you get a ten-minute break before the Extended Response (also known as the essay).

During the test, the computer will keep you constantly aware of the time with a clock in the upper right-hand corner. Pay attention to the clock. When the test begins, check that time, and be sure to monitor how much time you have left as you work your way through the test. Table 4-1 shows you how much time you have for each test.

Table 4-1	Time for Each GED Test
Test	**Time Limit (in Minutes)**
Reasoning Through Language Arts	95
Reasoning Through Language Arts, Extended Response	45
Social Studies	90
Science	90
Mathematical Reasoning	90

As you start, quickly scroll through the test and find out how many questions you have to answer. Quickly divide the time by the number of questions. Doing so can give you a rough idea of how much time to spend on each question. For example, on the Mathematical Reasoning section, suppose that you see you have 50 questions to answer. You have 90 minutes to complete the test. Divide the time by the number of questions to find out how much time you have for each item: 90/50 = 1.8 minutes per item. As you progress, repeat the calculation to see how you're doing. Remember, too, that you can do questions in any order, except for the Extended Response items. Do the easiest questions first. If you get stuck on a question, leave it and come back to it later, if you have time. Keeping to that schedule and answering as many questions as possible is essential.

As you can see from Table 4-1, if you don't monitor the time for each question, you won't have time to answer all the questions on the test. Keep in mind the following general time-management tips to help you complete each exam on time:

- ✔ **Measure the time you have to answer each question without spending more time on timing than answering.** Group questions together; for example, plan to do five questions in seven minutes. Doing so helps you complete all the questions and leaves you several minutes for review.

- ✔ **Keep calm and don't panic.** The time you spend panicking could be better spent answering questions.

- ✔ **Practice using the sample test sections in this book.** The more you practice timed sample test questions, the easier managing a timed test becomes. You can get used to doing something in a limited amount of time if you practice. Refer to the earlier section, "Using Practice Tests to Your Advantage" for more information.

When time is up, immediately stop and breathe a sigh of relief. When the test ends, the examiner will give you a log-off procedure. Listen for instructions on what to do or where to go next.

Evaluating the different questions

Although you don't have to know too much about how the test questions, or items, were developed to answer them correctly, you do need some understanding of how they're constructed. Knowing the types of items you're dealing with can make answering them easier — and you'll face fewer surprises.

To evaluate the types of questions that you have to answer, keep these tips in mind:

- ✔ **As soon as the computer signals that the test is running, start by skimming the questions.** Don't spend a lot of time doing so — just enough to spot the questions you absolutely know and the ones you know you'll need more time to answer.

- ✔ **Rely on the Previous and Next buttons on the bottom of the screen to scroll through the questions.** After you finish skimming, answer all the questions you know first; that way, you leave yourself much more time for the difficult questions. Check out the later section "Addressing and answering questions" for tips on how to answer questions.

- ✔ **Answer the easiest ones first.** You don't have to answer questions in order. Nobody except you will ever know, or care, in which order you answer the questions, so do the easiest questions first. You'll be able to answer them fastest, leaving more time for the other, harder, questions.

Knowing the question type can shape the way you think about the answer. Some questions ask you to analyze a passage or extract from a document, which means the information you need is in the source text. Others ask you to infer from the passage, which means that not all of the information is in the passage. Although none of the tests are labeled with the following titles, the GED test questions assess your skills in these areas.

Analysis

Analysis questions require you to break down information and look at how the information bits are related to one another. Analyzing information in this way is part of reasoning and requires you to

- ✔ **Separate facts from opinions.** Unless the text you're reading gives evidence or "proof" to support statements, treat them as opinion.

- ✔ **Realize that when an assumption isn't stated it may not necessarily be true.** Assumptions stated in the passage or question help you find the best answer.

- ✔ **Identify a cause-and-effect relationship.** For example, you have to eat an ice-cream cone quickly in hot weather. The cause is the hot weather and the effect is that the ice cream melts quickly.

- ✔ **Infer.** You may be asked to reach a conclusion based on evidence presented in the question. _Inferring_ is a fancy way of saying that you'll reach a conclusion. In the preceding example, you can infer that you should stay in an air-conditioned space to eat your ice cream or eat it very quickly.

- ✔ **Compare.** If you consider the similarities between ideas or objects, you're _comparing_ them. The world is like a basketball because both are round, for example.

- ✔ **Contrast.** If you consider the differences between ideas or objects, you're _contrasting_ them. For example, the world isn't like a basketball because it's so much larger and has an irregular surface.

Relating to other people in social situations exposes most people to these skills. For example, in most sports-related conversations between friends (or rivals), you quickly figure out how to separate fact from opinion and how to infer, compare, contrast, and identify cause-and-effect relationships. In other social situations, you come to realize when an assumption isn't stated. For example, you likely assume that your best friend or significant other is going to join you for a late coffee the night before an important test, but, in reality, your friend may be planning to go to bed early. Unstated assumptions you make can get you into trouble, both in life and on the GED test.

Application

Application questions require you to use the information presented to you in one situation to help you in a different situation. You've been applying information left and right for most of your life, but you probably don't realize it. For example, when you use the information from the morning newspaper to make a point in an argument in the afternoon, you use your application skills.

Comprehension

A *comprehension* question asks whether you understand written material. The GED test-makers expect you to be able to state the info on the test in your own words, develop a summary of the ideas presented, discuss the implications of those ideas, and draw conclusions from those implications. You need to develop these comprehension skills to understand what the questions are asking you and to answer the questions successfully.

The best way to increase your comprehension is to read extensively and to ask another person to ask you questions about what you read. You can also use commercial books that specifically help you with your comprehension by presenting you with written material and asking you questions about it. One of those books is in your hands. All the other *For Dummies* test-preparation books as well as *AP English Literature & Composition For Dummies,* by Geraldine Woods (Wiley), have reading comprehension as a major focus, too. Feel free to check out these books to improve your comprehension if you still have difficulty after using this book.

Synthesis

Synthesis questions require you to take apart blocks of information presented to you and put the pieces back together to form a hypothesis, theory, or story. Doing so gives you a new understanding or twist on the information that you didn't have before. Have you ever discussed something that happened, giving it your own twist and explanation to create a brand new narrative? If so, you've already put your synthesis skills to use.

Evaluation

Any time someone presents you with information or opinion, you judge it to make sure it rings true in your mind. This *evaluation* helps you make decisions about the information presented before you decide to use it. If the clerk behind the ice-cream counter suggests you get a raspberry cone instead of the flavor you wanted because everyone knows that raspberry melts slower than all the other flavors, you may be a bit suspicious. If you notice that the clerk also has four containers of raspberry ice cream and only one of each other flavor, you may evaluate it as biased or even incorrect.

Cognitive skills

Mental skills that you use to get knowledge are called *cognitive skills* and include reasoning, perception, and intuition. They're particularly important in reading for understanding, which is what you're asked to do on the GED test. You can increase your knowledge and comprehension by reading books, researching on the web, or watching documentaries. After you read or watch something new, discuss it with others to make sure you understand it and can use it in conversation.

Addressing and answering questions

When you start the test, you want to have a game plan in place for how to answer the questions. Keep the following tips in mind to help you address each question:

- **Whenever you read a question, ask yourself, "What am I being asked?"** Doing so helps you stay focused on what you need to find out to answer the question. You may even want to decide quickly what skills are required to answer the question (see the preceding section for more on these skills). Then try to answer it.

✔ **Try to eliminate some answers.** Even if you don't really know the answer, guessing can help. When you're offered four answer choices, some will be obviously wrong. Eliminate those choices, and you have already improved your odds of guessing a correct answer.

✔ **Don't overthink.** Because all the questions are straightforward, don't look for hidden or sneaky questions. The questions ask for an answer based on the information given. If you don't have enough information to answer the question, one of the answer choices will say so.

✔ **Find the best answer and quickly verify that it answers the question.** If it does, click on that choice, and move on. If it doesn't, leave it and come back to it after you answer all the other questions, if you have time. *Remember:* You need to pick the *most* correct answer from the choices offered. It may not be the perfect answer, but it is what is required.

Guess for success: Using intelligent guessing

The multiple-choice questions, regardless of the on-screen format, provide you with four possible answers. You get between one and three points for every correct answer. Nothing is subtracted for incorrect answers. That means you can guess on the items you don't know for sure without fear that you'll lose points. Make educated guesses by eliminating as many obviously wrong choices as possible and choosing from just one or two remaining choices.

When the question gives you four possible answers and you randomly choose one, you have a 25 percent chance of guessing the correct answer without even reading the question. Of course, we don't recommend using this method during the test.

If you know that one of the answers is definitely wrong, you now have just three answers to choose from and have a 33 percent chance (1 in 3) of choosing the correct answer. If you know that two of the answers are wrong, you leave yourself only two possible answers to choose from, giving you a 50 percent (1 in 2) chance of guessing right — much better than 25 percent! Removing two or three choices you know are wrong makes choosing the correct answer much easier.

If you don't know the answer to a particular question, try to spot the wrong choices by following these tips:

✔ **Make sure your answer really answers the question at hand.** Wrong choices usually don't answer the question — that is, they may sound good, but they answer a different question than the one the test asks.

✔ **When two answers seem very close, consider both answers carefully because they both can't be right — but they both *can* be wrong.** Some answer choices may be very close, and all seem correct, but there's a fine line between completely correct and nearly correct. Be careful. These answer choices are sometimes given to see whether you really understand the material.

✔ **Look for opposite answers in the hopes that you can eliminate one.** If two answers contradict each other, both can't be right, but both can be wrong.

✔ **Trust your instincts.** Some wrong choices may just strike you as wrong when you first read them. If you spend time preparing for these exams, you probably know more than you think.

Leaving time for review

Having a few minutes at the end of a test to check your work is a great way to set your mind at ease. These few minutes give you a chance to look at any questions that may be troubling. If you've chosen an answer for every question, enjoy the last few minutes before time is called — without any panic. Keep the following tips in mind as you review your answers:

- ✓ **After you know how much time you have per item, try to answer each item in a little less than that time.** The extra seconds you don't use the first time through the test add up for time at the end of the test to review. Some questions require more thought and decision making than others. Use your extra seconds to answer those questions.

- ✓ **Don't try to change a lot of answers at the last minute.** Second-guessing yourself can lead to trouble. Often, second-guessing leads you to changing correct answers to incorrect ones. If you have prepared well and worked numerous sample questions, then you're likely to get the correct answers the first time. Ignoring all your preparation and knowledge to play a hunch isn't a good idea, either at the race track or on a test.

- ✓ **On tests where you're required to write essays, use any extra time to reread and review your final essay.** You may have written a good essay, but you always need to check for typos and grammar mistakes. The essay is evaluated both for style, content, and proper English. That includes spelling and grammar.

Keeping Your Head in the Game

To succeed in taking the GED test, you need to be prepared. In addition to studying the content and skills needed for the four tests, you also want to be mentally prepared. Although you may be nervous, you can't let your nerves get the best of you. Stay calm and take a deep breath. Here are a few pointers to help you stay focused on the task at hand:

- ✓ **Take time to relax.** Passing the GED test is an important milestone in life. Make sure you leave a bit of time to relax, both while you prepare for the test and just before you take it. Relaxing has a place in preparing as long as it doesn't become your main activity.

- ✓ **Make sure you know the rules of the room before you begin.** If you have questions about using the bathroom during the test or what to do if you finish early, ask the proctor before you begin. If you don't want to ask these questions in public, call the GED office in your area before the test day, and ask your questions over the telephone. For general GED questions, call 800-62-MYGED or check out `www.gedtestingservice.com`.

- ✓ **Keep your eyes on your monitor.** Everybody knows not to look at other people's work during the test, but, to be on the safe side, don't stretch, roll your eyes, or do anything else that may be mistaken for looking at another test.

- ✓ **Stay calm.** Your nerves can use up a lot of energy needed for the test. Concentrate on the job at hand. You can always be nervous or panicky some other time.

Because taking standardized tests probably isn't a usual situation for you, you may feel nervous. This is perfectly normal. Just try to focus on answering one question at a time, and push any other thoughts to the back of your mind. Sometimes taking a few deep breaths can clear your mind; just don't spend a lot of time focusing on your breath. After all, your main job is to pass the GED test.

Part II
A Full-Length Practice GED Test

Top Five Ways to Duplicate the GED Test Environment

For best results, take the GED practice test under simulated GED test conditions by following these tips:

✔ Find a quiet place to work, where you won't be distracted or interrupted.

✔ Use the answer sheet provided and record your answers with a pencil.

✔ Set a timer to count down from the total time allocated for each section of the test.

✔ *Don't* go to the next section until the time allotted for the current section is up. If you finish early, check your work for that section only.

✔ Don't take a break during any test section; however, give yourself exactly one 10-minute break on the Reasoning Through Language Arts test before writing the Extended Response.

In this part. . .

✔ See how your stamina measures up by taking full-length GED practice test sections.

✔ Score your test quickly with the answer key.

✔ Discover how to improve your performance by reading through the answer explanations for all practice test questions.

Chapter 5

Section 1: Reasoning Through Language Arts

You're ready to take a crack at a full-blown practice GED Reasoning Through Language Arts test. You're feeling good and ready to go (well, maybe not, but you're at least smart enough to know that this practice is good for you).

You have 95 minutes to complete the two sections of short items and then another 45 minutes to write the Extended Response (a separate item). You get a 10-minute break after the first set of items and the Extended Response, and before starting on the second set of items. Remember, you can't save time from one section to use in the other.

The answers and explanations to this section's questions are in Chapter 9. Go through the explanations to all the questions, even for the ones you answered correctly. The explanations are a good review of the techniques we discuss throughout the book.

Unless you require accommodations, you'll be taking the GED test on a computer. Instead of marking your answers on a separate answer sheet, like you do for the practice test sections in this book, you'll see clickable ovals and fill-in-the-blank text boxes, and you'll be able to click with your mouse and drag and drop items where indicated. We formatted the questions and answer choices in this book to make them appear as similar as possible to what you'll see on the computer-based test, but we had to retain some A, B, C, D choices for marking your answers, and we provide an answer sheet for you to do so. Also, to make it simpler for you to time yourself, we present the short answer items in one unit, rather than two units, and the Extended Response (the essay) as a separate 45-minute section at the end of this chapter.

Answer Sheet for Section 1, Reasoning Through Language Arts

1. Ⓐ Ⓑ Ⓒ Ⓓ	31. Ⓐ Ⓑ Ⓒ Ⓓ
2. Ⓐ Ⓑ Ⓒ Ⓓ	32. Ⓐ Ⓑ Ⓒ Ⓓ
3. ▭	33. Ⓐ Ⓑ Ⓒ Ⓓ
4. Ⓐ Ⓑ Ⓒ Ⓓ	34. Ⓐ Ⓑ Ⓒ Ⓓ
5. Ⓐ Ⓑ Ⓒ Ⓓ	35. Ⓐ Ⓑ Ⓒ Ⓓ
6. Ⓐ Ⓑ Ⓒ Ⓓ	36. ▭
7. Ⓐ Ⓑ Ⓒ Ⓓ	37. ▭
8. Ⓐ Ⓑ Ⓒ Ⓓ	38. Ⓐ Ⓑ Ⓒ Ⓓ
9. Ⓐ Ⓑ Ⓒ Ⓓ	39. Ⓐ Ⓑ Ⓒ Ⓓ
10. Ⓐ Ⓑ Ⓒ Ⓓ	40. ▭
11. Ⓐ Ⓑ Ⓒ Ⓓ	41. Ⓐ Ⓑ Ⓒ Ⓓ
12. Ⓐ Ⓑ Ⓒ Ⓓ	42. ▭
13. Ⓐ Ⓑ Ⓒ Ⓓ	43. Ⓐ Ⓑ Ⓒ Ⓓ
14. Ⓐ Ⓑ Ⓒ Ⓓ	44. Ⓐ Ⓑ Ⓒ Ⓓ
15. Ⓐ Ⓑ Ⓒ Ⓓ	45. ▭
16. Ⓐ Ⓑ Ⓒ Ⓓ	46. Ⓐ Ⓑ Ⓒ Ⓓ
17. Ⓐ Ⓑ Ⓒ Ⓓ	47. Ⓐ Ⓑ Ⓒ Ⓓ
18. Ⓐ Ⓑ Ⓒ Ⓓ	48. Ⓐ Ⓑ Ⓒ Ⓓ
19. Ⓐ Ⓑ Ⓒ Ⓓ	49. Ⓐ Ⓑ Ⓒ Ⓓ
20. Ⓐ Ⓑ Ⓒ Ⓓ	50. ▭
21. Ⓐ Ⓑ Ⓒ Ⓓ	51. Ⓐ Ⓑ Ⓒ Ⓓ
22. Ⓐ Ⓑ Ⓒ Ⓓ	52. Ⓐ Ⓑ Ⓒ Ⓓ
23. Ⓐ Ⓑ Ⓒ Ⓓ	53. Ⓐ Ⓑ Ⓒ Ⓓ
24. ▭	54. ▭
25. Ⓐ Ⓑ Ⓒ Ⓓ	55. Ⓐ Ⓑ Ⓒ Ⓓ
26. ▭	56. Ⓐ Ⓑ Ⓒ Ⓓ
27. ▭	57. Ⓐ Ⓑ Ⓒ Ⓓ
28. Ⓐ Ⓑ Ⓒ Ⓓ	58. Ⓐ Ⓑ Ⓒ Ⓓ
29. Ⓐ Ⓑ Ⓒ Ⓓ	59. Ⓐ Ⓑ Ⓒ Ⓓ
30. Ⓐ Ⓑ Ⓒ Ⓓ	60. Ⓐ Ⓑ Ⓒ Ⓓ

Reasoning Through Language Arts Test

Time: 95 minutes

Directions: You may answer the questions in this section in any order. Mark your answers on the answer sheet provided by filling in the corresponding oval or writing your answer in the blank box.

Questions 1–5 refer to the following excerpt, written by Dale Shuttleworth (originally printed in the Toronto Star, *January 2008).*

What Is The History Of The Social Enterprise Movement?

Line The Center for Social Innovation, a renovated warehouse in the Spadina Ave. area of
Toronto, houses 85 "social enterprises," including organizations concerned with the environment, the arts, social justice, education, health, technology, and design. Tribute has
been paid to the "social enterprise movement" in Quebec and Vancouver for providing the
(05) impetus for this very successful venture.

Toronto, Ontario, also has provided leadership in the areas of community education and
community economic development — essential components in the creation of social enterprises. In 1974, the Toronto Board of Education assisted in the establishment of the Learnxs
Foundation Inc. as part of its Learning Exchange System.

(10) The foundation represented an additional source of support for the burgeoning "alternatives in education" movement. In 1973, the Ontario government had imposed ceilings on
educational spending and, together with reduced revenue due to declining enrollment, the
Toronto board had limited means to fund innovative and experimental programs. The
Learnxs Foundation was an independent "arms-length" nonprofit charitable enterprise,
(15) which could solicit funds from public and private sources and generate revenue through the
sale of goods and services to support innovative programs within the Toronto system.

What followed during the 1970s was a series of Learnxs-sponsored demonstration projects
as a source of research and development in such areas as: school and community programs
to improve inner-city education; a series of small enterprises to employ 14- to 15-year-old
(20) school leavers; Youth Ventures — a paper recycling enterprise employing at-risk youth;
Artsjunction — discarded material from business and industry were recycled for use as
craft materials for visual arts classes; Toronto Urban Studies Centre — a facility to encourage the use of the city as a learning environment; and Learnxs Press — a publishing house
for the production and sale of innovative learning materials.

(25) The York Board of Education and its school and community organizations jointly incorporated
the Learning Enrichment Foundation (LEF), modeled on Learnxs. Originally devoted to multicul-
tural arts enrichment, LEF during the 1980s joined with parental groups and the school board to
establish 13 school-based childcare centers for infants, pre-school and school-age children.

In 1984, LEF was asked by Employment and Immigrant Canada to convene a local committee
(30) of adjustment in response to York's high rate of unemployment and plant closures.
Outcomes of the work of the Committee included:

York Business Opportunities Centre: In 1985, with support from the Ontario Ministry of
Industry, Trade & Technology, LEF opened the first small business incubator operated by a
nonprofit charitable organization.

Go on to next page

(35) Microtron Centre: This training facility was devoted to micro-computer skills, word and numerical processing, computer-assisted design, graphics and styling, and electronic assembly and repair.

Microtron Bus: This refurbished school bus incorporated eight workstations from the Microtron Centre. It visited small business, industry and service organizations on a scheduled
(40) basis to provide training in word and numerical processing for their employees and clients.

In 1996, the Training Renewal Foundation was incorporated as a nonprofit charity to serve disadvantaged youth and other displaced workers seeking skills, qualifications and employment opportunities. Over the years, TRF has partnered with governments, employers and community organizations to provide a variety of services including job-creation programs
(45) for: immigrants and refugees, GED high school equivalency, café equipment technicians, coffee and vending service workers, industrial warehousing and lift truck operators, fully expelled students, youth parenting, construction craft workers and garment manufacturing.

1. The Center for Social Innovation is

   (A) a new restaurant

   (B) a center housing social enterprises

   (C) the head office of a charity

   (D) a small enterprise to employ school leavers

2. The Learnxs Foundation supported

   (A) homeless people

   (B) scholarships for computer studies students

   (C) innovative programs

   (D) art programming

3. Artsjunction specialized in [＿＿＿＿＿＿].

4. The Microtron bus helped

   (A) provide transportation for computer science students to their labs

   (B) provide training in word and numerical processing to employees and clients

   (C) train auto mechanics in the digital controls in the new cars

   (D) the center establish social enterprises

5. The Training Renewal Foundation serves

   (A) as a social innovator for youth

   (B) as a patron of the center

   (C) dinner to the homeless

   (D) as a business incubator

Questions 6–10 refer to the following excerpt.

How Must Employees Behave?

It is expected that employees behave in a respectful, responsible, professional manner. Therefore, each employee must do the following:

- Wear appropriate clothing and use safety equipment where needed.

- Refrain from the use and possession of alcohol and/or illicit drugs and associated paraphernalia throughout the duration of the work day.

- Refrain from associating with those who pass, use, and are under the influence of illicit drugs and/or alcohol.

- Address all other employees and supervisors with courtesy and respect, using non-offensive language.

- Accept the authority of supervisors without argument. If you consider an action unfair, inform the Human Resources department.

Go on to next page

- Respect the work environment of this company and conduct oneself in a manner conducive to the growth and the enhancement of our business.

- Refrain from inviting visitors to our place of work to keep the premises secure.

- Promote the dignity of all persons, regardless of gender, creed, or culture and conduct oneself with dignity.

If the employee chooses *not* to comply:

- On the first offense, the employee meets with his or her supervisor. A representative from Human Resources may choose to attend.

- On the second offense, the employee meets with the Vice President of Human Resources before returning to work.

- On the third offense, the employee is dismissed.

6. Which requirement relates to employee appearance?

   (A) The employee must refrain from using alcohol.

   (B) The employee must not use associated paraphernalia.

   (C) The employee must wear appropriate clothing.

   (D) The employee must use courtesy and respect.

7. Which requirement addresses relations with supervisors?

   (A) Accept authority.

   (B) Contribute to business growth and enhancement.

   (C) Use non-offensive language.

   (D) Do not use drugs and alcohol.

8. Which requirement is concerned with the growth and enhancement of the business?

   (A) conducive to growth

   (B) enhancement of self

   (C) dressing unprofessionally

   (D) personal conduct

9. How are safety and security protected?

   (A) by promoting dignity

   (B) by not inviting others in

   (C) by the types of interaction

   (D) through meetings with supervisors

10. What are the penalties for continued noncompliance?

    (A) You meet with the president of the company.

    (B) You must avoid your supervisor.

    (C) You have to take behavior classes.

    (D) You are fired.

Go on to next page

Questions 11–20 refer to the following business letter.

CanLearn Study Tours, Inc.
2500 Big Beaver Road
Troy, MI 70523

Dr. Dale Worth, Ph.D. Registrar
BEST Institute of Technology
75 Ingram Drive
Concord, MA 51234

Dear Dr. Worth:

(A)

(1) Our rapidly changing economic climate has meant both challenges never before known. (2) It has been said that only those organizations who can maintain loyalty and commitment among their employees, members, and customers will continue to survive and prosper in this age of continuous learning and globalization.

(B)

(3) Since 1974, CanLearn Study Tours, Inc. have been working with universities, colleges, school districts, voluntary organizations, and businesses to address the unique learning needs of their staff and clientele. (4) These have included educational travel programs that explore the following, artistic and cultural interests, historic and archeological themes, environmental and wellness experiences, and new service patterns. (5) Professional development strategies have been organized to enhance international understanding and boost creativity. (6) Some organizations' have used study tours to build and maintain their membership or consumer base. (7) Other organizations discover a new soarce of revenue in these difficult economic times.

(C)

(8) The formats have varied from a series of local seminars to incentive conferences or sales promotion meetings. (9) Our professional services, including the best possible transportation and accommodation at the most reasonable rates, have insured the success of these programs.

(D)

(10) We would appreciate the opportunity to share our experiences in educational travel and discuss the ways we may be of service to your organization.

Yours sincerely,

Todd Croft, M.A., President
CanLearn Study Tours, Inc.

Go on to next page

11. Sentence 1: **Our rapidly changing economic climate has meant both challenges never before known.**

    Which improvement should be made to Sentence 1?

    (A) insert *and opportunities* between *challenges* and *never*

    (B) change *has meant* to *have meant*

    (C) change *known* to *none*

    (D) no correction required

12. Sentence 2: **It has been said that only those organizations who can maintain loyalty and commitment among their employees, members, and customers will continue to survive and prosper in this age of continuous learning and globalization.**

    Which change should be made to Sentence 2?

    (A) insert a comma after *commitment*

    (B) change *has been* to *had been*

    (C) change *who* to *that*

    (D) change *those* to *these*

13. Sentence 3: **Since 1974, CanLearn Study Tours, Inc. have been working with universities, colleges, school districts, voluntary organizations, and businesses to address the unique learning needs of their staff and clientele.**

    Which is the best way to write the underlined portion of Sentence 3?

    (A) had been working

    (B) has been working

    (C) will be working

    (D) shall be working

14. Sentence 4: **These have included educational travel programs that explore the following, artistic and cultural interests, historic and archeological themes, environmental and wellness experiences, and new service patterns.**

    Which correction should be made to Sentence 4?

    (A) insert a comma after *have included*

    (B) change the comma after *following* to a colon

    (C) change the comma after *interests* to a colon

    (D) change the comma after *themes* to a colon

15. Sentence 5: **Professional development strategies have been organized to enhance international understanding and boost creativity.**

    Which change should be made to Sentence 5?

    (A) change *strategies* to *strategy*

    (B) change *boost* to *boast*

    (C) change *have been organized* to *has been organized*

    (D) no correction required

16. Sentence 6: **Some organizations' have used study tours to build and maintain their membership and consumer base.**

    Which correction should be made to Sentence 6?

    (A) change *organizations'* to *organizations*

    (B) change *Some* to *All*

    (C) change *their* to *there*

    (D) change *have used* to *has used*

17. Sentence 7: **Other organizations <u>discover a new soarce of revenue in these</u> difficult economic times.**

    Which change should be made to the underlined portion in Sentence 7?

    (A) discovering a new soarce of revenue in these

    (B) discover a new source of revenue in these

    (C) discover a new soarce, of revenue, in these

    (D) recover a new soarce of revenue in these

18. Sentence 8: **The formats has varied from a series of local seminars to incentive conferences or sales promotion meetings.**

    Which revision should be made to Sentence 8?

    (A) add a comma after *seminars*

    (B) add an apostrophe after *sales*

    (C) change *formats* to *format*

    (D) add a period after *seminars*

Go on to next page ➡

19. Sentence 9: **Our professional services, including the best possible transportation and accommodation at the most reasonable rates, have insured the success of these programs.**

    Which correction should be made to Sentence 9?

    (A) change *services* to *service*

    (B) replace *insured* with *ensured*

    (C) remove the comma after *services*

    (D) remove the comma after *rates*

20. Sentence 10: **We would appreciate the opportunity to share our experiences in educational travel and discuss the ways we may be of service to your organization.**

    Which revision should be made to Sentence 10?

    (A) change *would appreciate* to *appreciate*

    (B) insert a comma after *ways*

    (C) change *may* to *will*

    (D) no correction required

Questions 21–26 refer to the following excerpt from Washington Irving's "Rip Van Winkle" (1819).

What Can You Learn From The Mountains?

Line Whoever has made a voyage up the Hudson must remember the Kaatskill Mountains. They are a dismembered branch of the great Appalachian family, and are seen away to the west of the river, swelling up to a noble height, and lording it over the surrounding country. Every change of season, every change of weather, indeed, every hour of the (05) day, produces some change in the magical hues and shapes of these mountains, and they are regarded by all the good wives, far and near, as perfect barometers. When the weather is fair and settled, they are clothed in blue and purple, and print their bold outlines on the clear evening sky; but, sometimes, when the rest of the landscape is cloudless, they will gather a hood of gray vapors about their summits, which, in the (10) last rays of the setting sun, will glow and light up like a crown of glory.

At the foot of these fairy mountains, the voyager may have descried the light smoke curling up from a village, whose shingle-roofs gleam among the trees, just where the blue tints of the upland melt away into the fresh green of the nearer landscape. It is a little village of great antiquity, having been founded by some of the Dutch colonists, in (15) the early times of the province, just about the beginning of the government of the good Peter Stuyvesant, (may he rest in peace!) and there were some of the houses of the original settlers standing within a few years, built of small yellow bricks brought from Holland, having latticed windows and gablefronts, surmounted with weather-cocks.

21. How would you set out to find the Kaatskill Mountains?

    (A) Ask directions.

    (B) Journey up the Hudson.

    (C) Look for a dismembered branch.

    (D) Notice fresh green.

22. According to Lines 5 and 6, wives tell the weather

    (A) with perfect barometers

    (B) by the clear evening sky

    (C) through gray vapors

    (D) with magical hues and shapes

23. What clues might you look for as a sign that you are close to the village?

    (A) fairy mountains

    (B) shingle-roofs

    (C) light smoke curling

    (D) blue tints

24. Who originally founded the village?
    ☐☐☐☐☐☐

Go on to next page →

25. Why is the phrase "may he rest in peace!" (Line 16) used after Peter Stuyvesant?

    (A) He has since died.

    (B) He was an original settler.

    (C) He was a soldier.

    (D) He was the governor.

26. What materials came from Holland?

    [_____]

Questions 27–32 refer to the following excerpt from Richard Wright's "The Man Who Was Almost a Man," from Eight Men *(1961).*

What Do You Need To Be A Man?

Line   Dave struck out across the fields, looking homeward through paling light . . . One of these days he was going to get a gun and practice shooting, then they couldn't talk to him as though he were a little boy. He slowed, looking at the ground. Shucks, Ah ain scareda them . . . even ef they are biggern me! Aw, Ah know whut Ahma do. Ahm going
(05)   by ol Joe's sto n git that Sears-Roebuck catlog n look at them guns. Mebbe Ma will lemme buy one when she gits mah pay from ol man Hawkins. Ahma beg her t gimme some money. Ahm ol ernough to hava gun. Ahm seventeen. Almost a man. He strode, feeling his long loose-jointed limbs. Shucks, a man oughta hava little gun aftah he done worked hard all day.

(10)   He came in sight of Joe's store. A yellow lantern glowed on the front porch. He mounted steps and went through the screen door, hearing it bang behind him. There was a strong smell of coal oil and mackerel fish. He felt very confident until he saw fat Joe walk in through the rear door, then his courage began to ooze.

"Howdy, Dave! Whutcha want?"

(15)   "How yuh, Mistah Joe? Aw, Ah don wanna buy nothing. Ah jus wanted t see ef yuhd lemme look at tha catlog erwhile."

"Sure! You wanna see it here?"

"Nawsuh. Ah wants t take it home wid me. Ah'll bring it back termorrow when Ah come in from the fiels."

(20)   "You plannin on buying something?"

"Yessuh."

"Your ma lettin you have your own money now?"

"Shucks. Mistah Joe, Ahm gittin t be a man like anybody else!"

27. According to the story, Dave's place of employment was [_____].

28. Dave wanted "to get a gun" (Line 2) to

    (A) show he wasn't "scareda" the others

    (B) prove he wasn't unemployed

    (C) make his Ma proud

    (D) impress Joe

29. From where did Dave hope to get a gun?

    (A) from "Joe's sto"

    (B) from "ol man Hawkins"

    (C) from Ma

    (D) from the Sears-Roebuck "catlog"

Go on to next page ⟶

30. How would you find Joe's store at night?

    (A) by the smell of mackeral

    (B) by a yellow lantern glow

    (C) by the banging screen door

    (D) by the smell of coal oil

31. Why do you think Dave asked to take the catalog home?

    (A) He lost his nerve.

    (B) It was too dark to read.

    (C) He had to be home for supper.

    (D) He makes his own money.

32. What must Dave do to get the gun?

    (A) Find it in the catalog.

    (B) Convince Ma to give him the money.

    (C) Persuade Joe to place the order.

    (D) Get ol man Hawkins's permission.

Questions 33–42 refer to the following excerpt, which is adapted from Customer Service For Dummies, *by Karen Leland and Keith Bailey (Wiley).*

Fix the Problem

(1) This step requires you to listen to each customers assessment of the problem. (2) Your job when she explains the situation from her perspective is to fully absorb what she is saying about her unique set of circumstances. (3) After you identify the customer's problem, the next step, obviously, is to fix it. (4) Sometimes, you can easily remedy the situation by changing an invoice, redoing an order, waving or refunding charges, or replacing a defective product. (5) At other times fixing the problem is more complex because the damage or mistake cannot be repaired simply. (6) In these instances, mutually exceptable compromises need to be reached.

(7) Whatever the problem, this step begins to remedy the situation and gives the customer what she needs to resolve the source of the conflict. (8) Don't waste time and effort by putting the horse before the cart and trying to fix the wrong problem. (9) Its easy to jump the gun and think that you know what the customer is about to say because you've heard it all a hundred times before. (10) Doing so loses you ground on the recovery front and farther annoys the customer. (11) More often than not, what you think the problem is at first glance, is different from what it becomes upon closer examination.

33. Sentence 1: **This step requires <u>you to listen to each customers assessment</u> of the problem.**

    Which correction should be made to the underlined portion in Sentence 1?

    (A) you to listen each customers assessment

    (B) you to listen to each customers' assessment

    (C) you to listen to each customers asessment

    (D) you to listen to each customer's assessment

34. Sentence 2: **Your job when she explains the situation from her perspective is to fully absorb what she is saying about her unique set of circumstances.**

    To make Sentence 2 more effective, you may consider moving a section of the sentence, beginning with which group of words?

    (A) when she explains the situation from her perspective

    (B) Your job when she explains

    (C) what she is saying about

    (D) no correction required

Go on to next page

35. Sentence 4: **Sometimes, you can easily remedy the situation by changing an invoice, redoing an order, waving or refunding charges, or replacing a defective product.**

    Which correction should be made to Sentence 4?

    (A) change *redoing* to *re-doing*

    (B) change *invoice* to *invoise*

    (C) change *waving* to *waiving*

    (D) change *defective* to *defected*

36. Sentence 5: **At other times fixing the problem is more complex because the damage or mistake cannot be repaired simply.**

    After which word would it be most appropriate to place a comma? ☐

37. Sentence 6: **In these instances, mutually exceptable compromises need to be reached.**

    What one word is misspelled or misused in Sentence 6? ☐

38. Sentence 7: **Whatever the problem, this step begins to remedy the situation and gives the customer what she needs to resolve the source of the conflict.**

    Which is the best way to begin Sentence 7? If the original is the best way, choose Choice (A).

    (A) Whatever the problem,

    (B) This step begins to remedy,

    (C) What she needs to resolve,

    (D) To remedy the situation,

39. Sentence 8: **Don't waste time and effort by putting the horse before the cart and trying to fix the wrong problem.**

    Which change should be made to Sentence 8?

    (A) change *waste* to *waist*

    (B) revise to read *the cart before the horse*

    (C) change *trying* to *try*

    (D) change *Don't* to *Doesn't*

40. Sentence 9: **Its easy to jump the gun and think that you know what the customer is about to say because you've heard it all a hundred times before.**

    What word(s) is used incorrectly in Sentence 9? ☐

41. Sentence 10: **Doing so loses you ground <u>on the recovery front and farther</u> annoys the customer.**

    Which change should be made to the underlined portion in Sentence 10?

    (A) with the recovery front and farther

    (B) on the recover front and farther

    (C) on the recovery front and further

    (D) on the recovery, and farther

42. Sentence 11: **More often than not, what you think the problem is, at first glance, is different from what it becomes, upon closer examination.**

    The comma after which word is used correctly in Sentence 11? ☐

Questions 43–49 refer to the following business letter.

BEST Institute of Technology
75 Ingram Drive
Concord, MA 51234

To whom it may concern:

(1) I am pleased to comment on the relationship of our organization to Peta Jackson of the York Square Employment resource Center. (2) The BEST Institute of Technology has partnered with the York Square ERC in recruiting candidates for our Café Technician and Operator training programs since April 2002.

Go on to next page ⟩

(3) In support of the partnership, Peta provided the following services to our programs

- Set up information presentations as part of her job readiness seminars
- Distributed print materials
- Counseled applicants
- Expedited meetings with potential candidates
- Arranged five graduating ceremonies held at York Square ERC

(4) Peta has always been a strong advocate for our program, which has trained more than 50 technicians and operators during the past 18 months. (5) The fact that York Square was our primary source of referrals are a tribute to Peta's efforts. (6) She has, with a high degree of professional competence and efficiency, pursued her responsibilities. (7) On a personal level, it has been a joy to work with Peta and I wish her the very best in her future endeavors.

Dale Worth, Ph.D., Registrar

43. Sentence 1: **I am pleased to comment on the relationship of our organization to Peta Jackson of the York Square Employment resource Center.**

Which revision should be made to Sentence 1?

(A) change *to Peta Jackson* to *of Peta Jackson*

(B) change *pleased* to *please*

(C) change *resource* to *Resource*

(D) change *Center* to *Centre*

44. Sentence 2: **The BEST Institute of Technology has partnered with the York Square ERC in recruiting candidates for our Café Technician and Operator training programs since April 2002.**

Which is the best way to improve Sentence 2?

(A) move *since April 2002* to the start of the sentence

(B) change *has partnered* to *have partnered*

(C) change *with* to *between*

(D) change *in recruiting* to *while recruiting*

45. Sentence 3: **In support of the partnership, Peta provided the following services to our programs**

- **Set up information presentations as part of her job readiness seminars**
- **Distributed print materials**
- **Counseled applicants**
- **Expedited meetings with potential candidates**
- **Arranged five graduating ceremonies held at York Square ERC**

This sentence requires a colon. After which word should it be inserted? [＿＿＿＿＿]

46. Sentence 4: **Peta has always been a strong advocate for our program, which has trained more than 50 technicians and operators during the past 18 months.**

Which is the best way to write the underlined portion of this sentence? If the original is the best way, choose Choice (A).

(A) has always been

(B) always has been

(C) has been always

(D) have always been

Go on to next page ⇨

47. Sentence 5: **The fact that York Square was our primary source of referrals are a tribute to Peta's efforts.**

    Which correction should be made to Sentence 5?

    (A) change *Peta's* to *Petas'*

    (B) change *are* to *is*

    (C) change *was* to *were*

    (D) no correction required

48. Sentence 6: **She has, with a high degree of professional competence and efficiency, pursued her responsibilities.**

    Which revision should be made to Sentence 6?

    (A) move *with a high degree of professional competence and efficiency,* after *She*

    (B) move *, with a high degree of professional competence and efficiency,* after *pursued*

    (C) move *, with a high degree of professional competence and efficiency* to the end of the sentence after *responsibilities*

    (D) place *with a high degree of professional competence and efficiency,* at the front of the sentence before *She*

49. Sentence 7: **On a personal level, it has been a joy to work with Peta and I wish her the very best in her future endeavors.**

    Which improvement should be made to Sentence 7?

    (A) add a comma after *Peta*

    (B) change *endeavors* to *endeavours*

    (C) change *has been* to *have been*

    (D) move *on a personal level* to come after *Peta*

Questions 50–55 refer to the following excerpt from Saul Bellow's "Something to Remember Me By" (1990).

How Did It All Begin?

Line   It began like any other winter school day in Chicago — grimly ordinary. The temperature a few degrees above zero, botanical frost shapes on the window-pane, the snow swept up in heaps, the ice gritty and the streets, block after block, bound together by the iron of the sky. A breakfast of porridge, toast,
(05)   and tea. Late as usual, I stopped for a moment to look into my mother's sick-room. I bent near and said, "It's Louie, going to school." She seemed to nod. Her eyelids were brown, her face was much lighter. I hurried off with my books on a strap over my shoulder.

When I came to the boulevard on the edge of the park, two small men rushed
(10)   out of a doorway with rifles, wheeled around aiming upward, and fired at pigeons near the rooftop. Several birds fell straight down, and the men scooped up the soft bodies and ran indoors, dark little guys in fluttering white shirts. Depression hunters and their city game. Moments before, the police car had loafed by at ten miles an hour. The men had waited it out.

(15)   This had nothing to do with me. I mention it merely because it happened. I stepped around the blood spots and crossed into the park.

Go on to next page

50. What words from this passage best describe the appearance of a winter school day in Chicago? [＿＿＿＿＿]

51. What do you find out about the state of Louie's home life in Lines 5 and 6?

    (A) He ate porridge, toast, and tea.

    (B) He carried books on a strap.

    (C) His face was much lighter.

    (D) His mother was sick.

52. What were the men doing in the doorway?

    (A) hunting for game

    (B) having target practice

    (C) staying out of the weather

    (D) hiding from police

53. What is the importance of the term *depression hunters* in this passage?

    (A) It tells you the state of mind of the men.

    (B) A lot of people hunted in the Depression.

    (C) They were reacting to the grim weather.

    (D) It reinforces the image of great hardship, that people had to hunt pigeons for food in the cities.

54. What adjective from the passage best describes the hunters? [＿＿＿＿＿]

55. Why didn't Louie tell the police about what he saw?

    (A) He was in a hurry to get to school.

    (B) His mother was sick.

    (C) It had nothing to do with him.

    (D) The guys were his friends.

Questions 56–60 refer to the following excerpt from Russell Hart's Photography For Dummies, *2nd Edition (Wiley).*

What's The Secret To Loading Batteries?

Line   If you've ever had to figure out where to stick batteries in your child's latest electronic acquisition, then loading batteries in your point-and-shoot shouldn't be a challenge. Turn off your camera when you install them; the camera may go crazy opening and closing its lens. (Some cameras turn themselves off after

(05)   you install new batteries, so you have to turn them back on to shoot.)

With big point-and-shoot models, you typically open a latched cover on the bottom to install batteries. More compact models have a battery compartment under a door or flap that is incorporated into the side or grip of the camera. You may have to pry open such doors with a coin.

(10)   More annoying are covers on the bottom that you open by loosening a screw. (You need a coin for this type, too.) And most annoying are battery covers that aren't hinged and come off completely when you unscrew them. If you have one of these, don't change batteries while standing over a sewer grate, in a field of tall grass, or on a pier.

(15)   Whether loading four AAs or a single lithium, make sure that the batteries are correctly oriented as you insert them. You'll find a diagram and/or plus and minus markings, usually within the compartment or on the inside of the door.

If your camera doesn't turn on and the batteries are correctly installed, the batteries may have lost their punch from sitting on a shelf too long. Which is

(20)   where the battery icon comes in.

If your camera has an LCD panel, an icon tells you when battery power is low.

Go on to next page ⇒

56. Where will you be installing the batteries?

    (A) an electronic acquisition

    (B) a children's toy

    (C) a big point-and-shoot

    (D) a camera

57. What is the easiest model in which to replace the batteries?

    (A) compact models

    (B) big point-and-shoots

    (C) screw bottoms

    (D) covers not hinged

58. Why should locations such as sewer grates and tall grass be avoided when changing batteries?

    (A) Water can get in the camera.

    (B) Your lens may get dirty.

    (C) Your card might be ruined.

    (D) The battery cover may be lost.

59. How do you ensure that the batteries are correctly oriented?

    (A) Use four AAs.

    (B) Use a single lithium.

    (C) Empty the compartment.

    (D) Find a diagram.

60. What tells you whether the batteries are low?

    (A) the LCD panel

    (B) the battery icon

    (C) the battery compartment

    (D) a single lithium battery

The Extended Response

Time: 45 minutes

Your assignment: The following articles present arguments both for and against making cyberbullying a criminal offence.

In your response, analyze the positions presented in each article and explain which you think is best supported. You must use specific and appropriate evidence to support your arguments. Write your response on the pages provided.

Pro

Some youth deliberately set out to harm others by using social media, texting, and other technologies. That should be a crime, especially because the intent to hurt and harm is there. The resulting evidence of the harm is also clear. The number of young people who have in desperation committed suicide after months and years of horrific abuse shows that.

Cyberbullying is a form of abuse, just like cyberstalking. It relentlessly follows a designated target. In a recent case, a teen was raped, and photographs of the rape were distributed to classmates in her school. Comments that followed taunted her as a slut — it was her fault; she was asking for it — to the point that she transferred schools. The teen reported the rape to the police who took little action, and the perps remained free. She received an endless stream of abusive e-mails and text. Meetings with the principal of the high school solved nothing. Even after transferring, the bullies found her again and the harassment started again. The teen eventually committed suicide.

This was not an isolated case. Nearly half of all teens report they have been victims. There have been multiple suicides in many countries. The police are often unwilling or unable to take action, claiming that cyberbullying does not constitute a crime.

Education programs don't work. Virtually all schools these days have anti-bullying programs. Even grade school children are taught about bullying and respect for others. They are also educated on how to be safe online. Yet bullying continues.

The threat of a criminal record certainly would be a deterrent and, at the very least, give the police a tool with which to fight cyberbullying. It might also give the victims a tool for seeking redress from the bullies. All the other initiatives have failed, so what choice is left?

Against

There are several considerations in the debate on criminalizing cyberbullying. There are already laws against cyberbullying, if it crosses the line into criminal harassment. That is a chargeable offence. Second, how can one keep a clear line between cyberbullying and an abrogation of the freedom of speech guaranteed by the Constitution? Further, does the threat of a criminal record really deter people from such activities?

The whole issue is unclear: How do you define cyberbullying? Mostly, it consists of wild accusations and name-calling. However, that is neither slanderous nor libellous, hence not a crime. If there is no physical harm done, and no intent to drive someone to self-harm, is verbal abuse a crime? When it continues and crosses into destruction of reputation, it does become criminal harassment. While this may be interpreted differently in different jurisdictions, it is a criminal offence. Existing laws can deal with this issue.

There are other tools. A young teen texted nude photos of her boyfriend's ex-girlfriend to friends. She also posted a copy on the former girlfriend's Facebook page. All were minors at the time. She was recently convicted of distributing child pornography, even though she, too, was a minor at the time. Existing laws punished the crime.

The other issue often raised is that cyberbullying has driven victims to suicide or attempts at self-harm. This is certainly true, but what is not proven is that the cyberbullying was the cause. Were the victims already suffering from depression? Were there other issues in their lives that made them unstable and prone to self-harm?

Proponents argue that the fear of a criminal charge will be a deterrent. But if that is the case, why do so many people still drive while drunk or continue to indulge in recreational drugs? There are clear consequences if caught, but they certainly do not stop these incidents.

The Constitution guarantees the right to free speech. When the law tries to tell people they cannot say something, at what point does that infringe on that right? Some social media have taken a solid first step. They no longer permit people to have accounts in false names.

Education is a better approach. Let's get the schools and parents, community groups, and churches all involved in teaching our teens to have respect for others. Teach teens that words can hurt, and that hurting others is never an appropriate thing to do.

STOP DO NOT TURN THE PAGE UNTIL TOLD TO DO SO.
DO NOT RETURN TO A PREVIOUS TEST.

Chapter 6

Section 2: Social Studies

• •

The Social Studies section consists of questions that measure general social studies concepts. The questions are based on short readings that often include a map, graph, chart, cartoon, or figure. Study the information given and then answer the question(s) following it. Refer to the information as often as necessary in answering the questions.

The Social Studies section of the GED test consists of two parts. You have about 65 minutes to complete the question-answer portion of the Social Studies component and about another 25 minutes to complete the Extended Response (the essay). *Note:* You have a total of 90 minutes to complete the entire Social Studies test; the time is one block, and you can allocate it any way you like. Work carefully, but don't spend too much time on any one item. Be sure you answer every item.

The answers and explanations to this section's questions are in Chapter 9. Go through the explanations to all the questions, even for the ones you answered correctly. The explanations are a good review of the techniques we discuss throughout the book.

Unless you require accommodations, you'll be taking the GED test on a computer. Instead of marking your answers on a separate answer sheet, like you do for the practice test sections in this book, you'll see clickable ovals and fill-in-the-blank text boxes, and you'll be able to click with your mouse and drag and drop items where indicated. We formatted the questions and answer choices in this book to make them appear as similar as possible to what you'll see on the computer-based test, but we had to retain some A, B, C, D choices for marking your answers, and we provide an answer sheet for you to do so.

Answer Sheet for Section 2, Social Studies

1. Ⓐ Ⓑ Ⓒ Ⓓ
2. Ⓐ Ⓑ Ⓒ Ⓓ
3. Ⓐ Ⓑ Ⓒ Ⓓ
4. Ⓐ Ⓑ Ⓒ Ⓓ
5. Ⓐ Ⓑ Ⓒ Ⓓ
6. Ⓐ Ⓑ Ⓒ Ⓓ
7. Ⓐ Ⓑ Ⓒ Ⓓ
8. Ⓐ Ⓑ Ⓒ Ⓓ
9. Ⓐ Ⓑ Ⓒ Ⓓ
10. Ⓐ Ⓑ Ⓒ Ⓓ
11. _____
12. Ⓐ Ⓑ Ⓒ Ⓓ
13. Ⓐ Ⓑ Ⓒ Ⓓ
14. _____
15. Ⓐ Ⓑ Ⓒ Ⓓ
16. Ⓐ Ⓑ Ⓒ Ⓓ
17. Ⓐ Ⓑ Ⓒ Ⓓ
18. Ⓐ Ⓑ Ⓒ Ⓓ
19. Ⓐ Ⓑ Ⓒ Ⓓ
20. _____
21. Ⓐ Ⓑ Ⓒ Ⓓ
22. Ⓐ Ⓑ Ⓒ Ⓓ
23. _____

24. Ⓐ Ⓑ Ⓒ Ⓓ
25. Ⓐ Ⓑ Ⓒ Ⓓ
26. Ⓐ Ⓑ Ⓒ Ⓓ
27. Ⓐ Ⓑ Ⓒ Ⓓ
28. ☐ ☐ ☐ ☐
29. Ⓐ Ⓑ Ⓒ Ⓓ
30. Ⓐ Ⓑ Ⓒ Ⓓ
31. Ⓐ Ⓑ Ⓒ Ⓓ
32. Ⓐ Ⓑ Ⓒ Ⓓ
33. _____
34. Ⓐ Ⓑ Ⓒ Ⓓ
35. Ⓐ Ⓑ Ⓒ Ⓓ
36. _____
37. Ⓐ Ⓑ Ⓒ Ⓓ
38. Ⓐ Ⓑ Ⓒ Ⓓ
39. Ⓐ Ⓑ Ⓒ Ⓓ
40. _____
41. Ⓐ Ⓑ Ⓒ Ⓓ
42. Ⓐ Ⓑ Ⓒ Ⓓ
43. Ⓐ Ⓑ Ⓒ Ⓓ
44. Ⓐ Ⓑ Ⓒ Ⓓ
45. Ⓐ Ⓑ Ⓒ Ⓓ

Social Studies Test

Time: 65 minutes

Directions: Mark your answers on the answer sheet provided by filling in the corresponding oval or writing your answer in the blank box.

Questions 1–5 refer to the following passage, which is excerpted from
CliffsQuickReview U.S. History I, *by P. Soifer and A. Hoffman (Wiley).*

Industry and Trade in the Thirteen Colonies

The colonies were part of an Atlantic trading network that linked them with England, Africa, and the West Indies. The pattern of commerce, not too accurately called the Triangular Trade, involved the exchange of products from colonial farms, plantations, fisheries, and forests with England for manufactured goods and the West Indies for slaves, molasses, and sugar. In New England, molasses and sugar were distilled into rum, which was used to buy African slaves. Southern Europe was also a valuable market for colonial foodstuffs.

Colonial industry was closely associated with trade. A significant percentage of Atlantic shipping was on vessels built in the colonies, and shipbuilding stimulated other crafts, such as the sewing of sails, milling of lumber, and manufacturing of naval stores. Mercantile theory encouraged the colonies to provide raw materials for England's industrializing economy; pig iron and coal became important exports. Concurrently, restrictions were placed on finished goods. For example, Parliament, concerned about possible competition from colonial hatters, prohibited the export of hats from one colony to another and limited the number of apprentices in each hatmaker's shop.

1. What did England, Africa, and the West Indies have in common?

   (A) They all had fisheries.

   (B) They all bought slaves.

   (C) They all distilled rum.

   (D) They all exchanged products.

2. What was rum used for?

   (A) colonial farms

   (B) milling of lumber

   (C) purchase of slaves

   (D) molasses and sugar

3. Why were the colonies important to Atlantic trade?

   (A) They built the ships.

   (B) They sewed sails.

   (C) They had naval stores.

   (D) They milled lumber.

4. How did the colonies support British industry?

   (A) They took part in sewing.

   (B) They produced finished goods.

   (C) They developed mercantile theory.

   (D) They provided raw materials.

5. What product was threatened by colonial competition?

   (A) coal

   (B) pig iron

   (C) hats

   (D) lumber

Go on to next page ⟹

Questions 6–11 refer to the following passage, which is excerpted from *The Declaration of Independence, 1776.*

Charges against the King

He has forbidden his governors to pass laws of immediate and pressing importance, unless suspended in their operation till his assent should be obtained; and when so suspended, he has utterly neglected to attend to them.

He has refused to pass other laws for the accommodation of large districts of people, unless those people would relinquish the right of representation in the legislature — a right inestimable to them, and formidable to tyrants only.

He has called together legislative bodies at places unusual, uncomfortable, and distant from the depository of their public records, for the sole purpose of fatiguing them into compliance with his measures.

He has dissolved representative houses repeatedly, for opposing, with manly firmness, his invasions on the rights of the people.

He has refused, for a long time after such dissolutions, to cause others to be elected; whereby the legislative powers, incapable of annihilation, have returned to the people at large, for their exercise, the state remaining in the meantime exposed to all the dangers of invasion from without, and convulsions within.

He has endeavored to prevent the population of these states; for that purpose obstructing the laws for naturalization of foreigners; refusing to pass others to encourage their migration hither, and raising the conditions of new appropriations of lands.

He has obstructed the administration of justice, by refusing his assent to laws for establishing judiciary powers.

He has made judges dependent on his will alone, for the tenure of their offices, and the amount and payment of their salaries.

He has erected a multitude of new offices, and sent hither swarms of officers, to harass our people, and eat out their substance.

He has kept among us, in times of peace, standing armies, without the consent of our legislature.

He has affected to render the military independent of, and superior to, the civil power.

6. The king neglected the colonies in many ways, especially by

   (A) failing to provide money

   (B) failing to pass laws

   (C) removing their right of condemnation

   (D) giving power to his governors

7. Which of the listed methods did the king use in an attempt to enforce compliance by legislative bodies to his wishes?

   (A) He never called them together.

   (B) He made them comfortable.

   (C) He made sure they were well rested.

   (D) He made them comply with his wishes.

Go on to next page

8. The main measure used by the king that was seen as a threat to the colonists' rights was

    (A) He dissolved representative houses.

    (B) He abdicated the throne.

    (C) He annihilated them.

    (D) He returned them to the people.

9. The king was very concerned about the growth of the colonies, so much so that he

    (A) gave away free land to people willing to settle

    (B) encouraged people to settle

    (C) settled there himself

    (D) discouraged people from settling

10. How did the king obstruct the judicial system?

    (A) He made it independent of his authority.

    (B) He erected new offices.

    (C) He refused to enact certain laws.

    (D) He harassed the people.

11. What was one way the freedom of the people was threatened? [   ]

Questions 12–13 refer to this map.

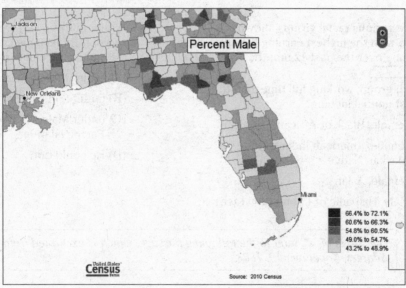

Illustration courtesy of the United States Census Bureau

---

12. People tend to live in areas with employment opportunities. Look at the areas with the lowest male population density. In these areas, the tourist industry is very important. Based on that information, what factors might explain lower male population density?

    (A) Tourist areas have more service-industry jobs, which are mostly female.

    (B) Because women have a greater life expectancy, there would be more elderly female tourists.

    (C) Men dislike working in the tourist industry.

    (D) Insufficient information is provided.

13. If the area shaded white around Miami has a population of 5.6 million people, approximately how many more females are there in the population than males?

    (A) 2.7 million

    (B) 2.9 million

    (C) 400,000

    (D) 1.2 million

Go on to next page

Questions 14–16 are based on this chart.

Median Earnings in the Past 12 Months
(In 2012 inflation-adjusted dollars)
by Sex by Work Experience in the Past 12 Months for the Population 16 Years And Over With Earnings in the Past 12 Months

San Francisco County, California
Powered by The American Community Survey

	One Race						Two or more races	
	White	Black or African American	American Indian and Alaska Native	Asian	Native Hawaiian and Other Pacific Islander	Some Other Race		Hispanic or Latino (any race)
Total:	$53,498	$31,149	$25,812	$36,052	$39,788	$23,678	$35,833	$27,016
Male	$60,910	$33,915	$27,766	$39,346	$48,347	$26,758	$37,400	$28,456
Worked full-time, year-round in the past 12 months	$79,234	$50,612	$48,393	$53,662	$62,896	$40,498	$62,516	$39,364
Other	$21,078	$15,787	$10,475	$14,320	$21,836	$13,581	$11,758	$13,423
Female	$47,729	$26,962	$17,365	$32,893	$31,386	$18,692	$33,719	$25,012
Worked full-time, year-round in the past 12 months	$65,675	$43,345	$34,205	$49,539	$43,185	$35,451	$56,736	$40,099
Other	$18,681	$10,280	$8,243	$13,428	$13,108	$10,831	$12,244	$11,741

Illustration courtesy of the United States Census Bureau

14. Of the various racial groups shown, the group with the highest earning if employed full-time over the past 12 months was _____.

15. Which group, working full time, had the lowest annual income?

  (A) Female, Black or African American

  (B) Female, American Indian and Alaskan Native

  (C) Female, Asian

  (D) Male, Hispanic or Latino (any race)

16. Where in this chart would a 15-year-old male of Chinese background find statistical information about his income group?

  (A) under Male, Asian

  (B) under Some Other Race

  (C) under Male, Native Hawaiian and Other Pacific Islander

  (D) He could not.

Questions 17–22 refer to the following passage, which is excerpted from Lincoln's Gettysburg Address, November 19, 1863.

Gettysburg Address

Four score and seven years ago, our fathers brought forth upon this continent a new nation, conceived in liberty and dedicated to the proposition that all men are created equal. Now we are engaged in a great civil war, testing whether that nation or any nation so conceived and so dedicated can long endure. We are met on a great battlefield of that war. We have come to dedicate a portion of that field as a final resting place for those who here gave their lives that that nation might live. It is altogether fitting and proper that we should do this. But, in a larger sense, we cannot dedicate, we cannot consecrate, we cannot hallow this ground. The brave men, living and dead, who struggled here have consecrated it far above our poor power to add or detract. The world will little note nor long remember what we say here, but it can never forget what they did here. . . .

Go on to next page

17. The issue of primary importance in this great civil war is

    (A) happiness and friendship

    (B) safety and security

    (C) liberty and equality

    (D) peace and prosperity

18. Where was President Lincoln's speech delivered?

    (A) on a train

    (B) at the White House

    (C) on a battlefield

    (D) on the radio

19. What does "little note nor long remember" mean?

    (A) The audience is not taking notes.

    (B) Lincoln has a bad memory.

    (C) The soldiers are not there to hear the speech.

    (D) People around the world will not remember the speech.

20. According to the address, a portion of the battlefield is used for ⬚⬚⬚⬚⬚⬚⬚.

21. Who has "hallow[ed] this ground"?

    (A) President Lincoln

    (B) those who fought there

    (C) the Confederate government

    (D) the Union government

22. What does "four score and seven" probably refer to?

    (A) soldiers

    (B) consecration

    (C) time

    (D) the war

Questions 23–28 refer to the following passage, which is excerpted from CliffsQuickReview U.S. History II, *by P. Soifer and A. Hoffman (Wiley).*

Causes of World War I

On June 28, 1914, a Serbian nationalist assassinated the Archduke Franz Ferdinand, the heir to the throne of Austria-Hungary. Austria demanded indemnities from Serbia for the assassination. The Serbian government denied any involvement with the murder and, when Austria issued an ultimatum, turned to its ally, Russia, for help. When Russia began to mobilize its army, Europe's alliance system, ironically intended to maintain the balance of power on the continent, drew one country after another into war. Austria's ally, Germany, declared war on Russia on August 1 and on France (which was allied with Russia) two days later. Great Britain entered the war on August 4, following Germany's invasion of neutral Belgium. By the end of August 1914, most of Europe had chosen sides: the Central Powers — Germany, Austria-Hungary, Bulgaria, and the Ottoman Empire (Turkey) — were up against the Allied Powers — principally Great Britain, France, Russia, and Serbia. Japan joined the Allied cause in August 1914, in hopes of seizing German possessions in the Pacific and expanding Japanese influence in China. This action threatened the Open Door Policy and led to increased tensions with the United States. Originally an ally of Germany and Austria-Hungary, Italy entered the war in 1915 on the side of Britain and France because they had agreed to Italian territorial demands in a secret treaty (the Treaty of London).

Go on to next page ⟹

23. The assassin of Archduke Ferdinand came from the country of ⬚⬚⬚⬚⬚.

24. Austria initially reacted to the assassination by

    (A) denying any involvement

    (B) demanding indemnities

    (C) asking for Russian help

    (D) declaring war

25. Which countries were not allies?

    (A) Serbia and Russia

    (B) Austria and Hungary

    (C) Germany and France

    (D) France and Great Britain

26. What caused Great Britain to enter the war?

    (A) Germany invaded Belgium.

    (B) Russia attacked Serbia.

    (C) Germany declared war on France.

    (D) Austria invaded Hungary.

27. Which country was not an Allied Power?

    (A) Great Britain

    (B) France

    (C) Germany

    (D) Serbia

28. Place the events in the proper sequence.

    (A) Italy enters on the Allied side.

    (B) Germany declares war on Russia.

    (C) Great Britain declares war on Germany.

    (D) Germany invades Belgium.

Questions 29–32 refer to the following political cartoon.

Illustration by Ricardo Checa

Go on to next page

29. How is President Barack Obama portrayed in the cartoon?

    (A) stand-up comedian

    (B) inspiring teacher

    (C) stern disciplinarian

    (D) fashion model

30. What do the smiling faces of the students symbolize?

    (A) happy voters

    (B) a receptive public

    (C) the bright future the President is hoping for

    (D) issues that can be solved

31. Why are two issues written in much smaller print on the spines of two textbooks?

    (A) These issues are very important but often overlooked.

    (B) These issues are less important.

    (C) Not enough room to draw more students.

    (D) They are just decoration.

32. What problems are the students facing in the future?

    (A) unemployment

    (B) shortage of energy

    (C) escalating debt

    (D) all of the above

Questions 33–36 refer to this table.

Table 852. Selected Farm Products—U.S. and World Production and Exports: 2000 to 2010

[In metric tons, except as indicated (60.6 represents 60,600,000). Metric ton = 1.102 short tons or .984 long tons]

Commodity	Unit	Amount						United States as percent of world		
		United States			World					
		2000	2005	2010	2000	2005	2010	2000	2005	2010
PRODUCTION [1]										
Wheat	Million	60.6	57.2	60.1	583.1	619.1	648.1	10.4	9.2	9.3
Corn for grain.	Million	251.9	282.3	316.2	591.4	699.7	815.3	42.6	40.3	38.8
Soybeans.	Million	75.1	83.5	90.6	175.8	220.7	262.0	42.7	37.8	34.6
Rice, milled	Million	5.9	7.1	7.6	399.4	418.2	451.6	1.5	1.7	1.7
Cotton [2]	Million bales [3]	17.2	23.9	18.1	89.1	116.4	114.6	19.3	20.5	15.8
EXPORTS [4]										
Wheat [5]	Million	28.9	27.3	34.7	101.5	117.0	124.7	28.5	23.3	27.8
Corn.	Million	49.3	54.2	48.3	76.9	81.1	90.6	64.2	66.9	53.2
Soybeans.	Million	27.1	25.6	42.2	53.7	63.4	95.6	50.5	40.3	44.1
Rice, milled basis.	Million	2.6	3.7	3.6	24.1	29.7	31.4	10.7	12.3	11.3
Cotton [2]	Million bales [3]	6.7	17.7	15.5	26.2	44.9	37.0	25.7	39.4	41.9

[1] Production years vary by commodity. In most cases, includes harvests from July 1 of the year shown through June 30 of the following year. [2] For production and trade years ending in year shown. [3] Bales of 480 lb. net weight. [4] Trade years may vary by commodity. Wheat, corn, and soybean data are for trade year beginning in year shown. Rice data are for calendar year. [5] Includes wheat flour on a grain equivalent.

Source: U.S. Department of Agriculture, Foreign Agricultural Service, "Production, Supply and Distribution Online," <http://www.fas.usda.gov/psdonline/psdhome.aspx>.

Illustration courtesy of the United States Department of Agriculture

33. What percentage of the world's soybean production came from the United States in 2010? ⬚

34. In 2010, approximately how much of the U.S. production of cotton was exported?

    (A) all of it

    (B) most of it

    (C) just under half

    (D) almost none

35. Between 2000 and 2010, world exports of corn

    (A) increased

    (B) decreased

    (C) decreased a lot

    (D) stayed about the same

36. What is the weight of a bale of cotton, according to the table? ⬚

Go on to next page ⟶

Questions 37–41 refer to the following timeline.

Timeline of Major Events in U.S. History

1900: Gold standard for currency adopted by United States.

1914: World War I begins.

1918: World War I ends.

1929: Stock market crashes; Great Depression begins.

1933: Gold exports banned; daily price established; U.S. citizens ordered to turn in all gold.

1934: Price of gold fixed at $35 per troy ounce.

1939: World War II begins.

1945: World War II ends.

1950: Korean Conflict begins.

1953: Korean Conflict ends.

1965: Vietnam War begins.

1973: Vietnam War ends; gold prices allowed to float; U.S. currency removed from gold standard.

1974: U.S. citizens allowed to own gold again.

1979: Soviet Union invades Afghanistan; U.S. hostages seized in Iran.

1980: Historic high prices for gold.

1987: Stock market crashes.

1989: Berlin Wall falls.

1990: Gulf War begins.

1991: Gulf War ends.

2001: Terrorist attacks on the United States.

2002: Invasion of Afghanistan and Iraq.

2008: United States elects first black president.

2009: United States slips into a recession.

Go on to next page

37. In 1900, the value of the United States' dollar was based on

    (A) stock market

    (B) value of gold

    (C) value of silver

    (D) trade surplus

38. What, if anything, is the connection between the stock market crash and the Great Depression in 1929?

    (A) It was the trigger.

    (B) Very little; economic problems had been building for some time before the crash.

    (C) Pure coincidence.

    (D) The stock market crash actually delayed the Great Depression.

39. What does "U.S. citizens ordered to turn in all gold" mean?

    (A) Citizens got to keep their gold.

    (B) Citizens had to tell the government about their gold.

    (C) Citizens could buy gold from each other, for profit.

    (D) Citizens had to take all their gold to government offices.

40. When was U.S. currency removed from the gold standard? [   ]

41. Based on what you see in the timeline, what likely caused the price of gold to reach an historic high?

    (A) Citizens were allowed to hold bullion.

    (B) Gold stocks were sold.

    (C) The Soviet Union invaded Afghanistan.

    (D) The Gulf War began.

Questions 42–44 refer to the following newscast.

World Environmental News

Good evening and welcome to World Environmental News.

Our stories this evening: cyclones in Korea, hurricane near Mexico, flooding in Europe and India, volcanic eruptions in New Guinea, drought in Australia, tornadoes in the United States, hailstorms in Italy, earthquakes in Iran, and locusts in Denmark.

Now, let's look at our top stories.

Drought in Australia: The wheat fields west of Canberra, New South Wales, are in great danger today because of the ongoing drought. In the next week, farmers may have to write off this year's crop, and this will likely lead to financial ruin for many of them. To add to the misery, hundreds of thousands of sheep had to be sold because there was not enough water for them to drink.

Locusts in Denmark: The unseasonably warm weather in Denmark is proving to be inviting to the lowly locust. Normally found along the Mediterranean coast, the locust has been found far from its normal habitat. These discoveries in southwest Denmark are causing concern because locusts have not been seen in Denmark for more than 50 years.

Hurricane near Mexico: Hurricane Herman is losing force off the Pacific coast of Mexico. The country is giving a sigh of relief as the hurricane winds down.

For wine drinkers: And a last note for you wine drinkers. The recent violent hailstorms in Italy are expected to cause a poor grape harvest. This means lower wine production and, consequently, higher prices.

There's more as nature lashes out. Tune in again for World Environmental News.

Go on to next page

42. The newscast says "cyclones in Korea, hurricane near Mexico"; what is the difference between cyclones and hurricanes?

    (A) Location. Meteorologists call these storms hurricanes in the Atlantic and northeast Pacific and cyclones in the eastern Pacific and Indian Ocean.

    (B) Cyclones are a form of tornado.

    (C) Cyclones are much more severe.

    (D) Unlike hurricanes, cyclones are always associated with flooding.

43. How does extreme drought cause financial problems for farmers?

    (A) Farmers lose their entire year's crop and income.

    (B) Selling off large herds of sheep at once leads to much lower prices and fewer sheep for future breeding stock.

    (C) There may be a minor problem, but crop insurance covers these losses.

    (D) Choices A and B.

44. Why is the finding of locusts in Denmark significant?

    (A) They reinforce the idea of climate change and global warming.

    (B) Prevailing winds have shifted.

    (C) Foreign ships carried insects and need more stringent inspection.

    (D) It is an isolated incident and has no real significance.

Question 45 refers to the following passage, taken from `www.cia.gov`.

By the time World War I started in 1914, the United States' ability to collect foreign intelligence had shrunk drastically because of budget cuts and bureaucratic reorganizations in the government. The State Department began small-scale collections against the Central Powers in 1916, but it wasn't until the United States declared war on Germany in 1917 that Army and Navy intelligence finally received more money and personnel. By that time, it was too late to increase their intelligence output to aid the cause very much.

The most significant advance for US intelligence during the war was the establishment of a permanent communications intelligence agency in the Army, what would become the forerunner of the National Security Agency. Meanwhile, the Secret Service, the New York Police Department, and military counterintelligence aggressively thwarted numerous German covert actions inside the United States, including psychological warfare, political and economic operations, and dozens of sabotage attempts against British-owned firms and factories supplying munitions to Britain and Russia.

45. How effective was U.S. foreign intelligence gathering during World War I?

    (A) Very effective; it stopped much domestic sabotage.

    (B) Not very effective; it depended on the New York Police Department.

    (C) It was limited because of pre-war budget cuts.

    (D) It was excellent at psychological warfare.

The Extended Response

Time: 25 minutes

Your assignment: Develop an argument on how the following passage reflects an enduring issue in American history. (***Note:*** An enduring issue is one that "reflects the founding principles of the United States and is an important idea that people often grapple with as new situations arise" [GED.com].) Incorporate material from the passage, the 14th Amendment, and your own knowledge of the enduring issues and the controversy surrounding this specific issue to support your argument.

14th Amendment of the Constitution of the United States

Section 1. *All persons born or naturalized in the United States, and subject to the jurisdiction thereof, are citizens of the United States and of the State wherein they reside. No State shall make or enforce any law which shall abridge the privileges or immunities of citizens of the United States; nor shall any State deprive any person of life, liberty, or property, without due process of law; nor deny to any person within its jurisdiction the equal protection of the laws.*

The Defense of Marriage Act (DOMA), passed in 1996, made it possible for state governments to refuse to recognize same-sex marriage granted in other jurisdictions. Section 3 of the Act made it impossible for same-sex couples to receive spousal benefits and any other federal benefits, from health insurance to social security benefits. That section was ruled unconstitutional in 2013. The second section of DOMA continues to exist. It exempts states, tribes, and possessions of the United States from the Constitutional requirements to recognize marriages formalized in another state. Any state can refuse to recognize same-sex marriages formalized elsewhere. The Constitution guarantees that marriages performed in any state are recognized in every other state, but the remnants of DOMA grant states an exemption on same-sex marriage.

For the lesbian, gay, bisexual, and transgender (LGBT) community, this means that discrimination remains in effect in numerous states that have not made same-sex marriage legal. Discrimination of any kind is in theory inappropriate, and yet the continuation of the second section of the Defense of Marriage Act allows it. This, too, is in direct violation of Section 1 of the 14th Amendment. Further, there are no federal laws that prohibit discrimination based on sexual orientation, and in any case, they generally would not apply to the private sector or religious organizations. More than half of the states have no prohibitions against discrimination based on sexual orientation or identity.

There has been obvious progress. The military has ended the policy of "Don't ask, don't tell" and ended discrimination based on sexual orientation. Some states now allow same-sex marriages and more have some degree of legal protections against discrimination based on sexual orientation. Discrimination based on sexual orientation is not permitted in federal health care programs, and there is some limited protection under federal hate crime laws. The Equal Employment Opportunity Commission ruled in 2011 and again in 2012 that job discrimination based on sexual orientation also is a form of discrimination covered by the Civil Rights Act of 1964. Despite all these changes, there is much left to do.

To be a nation truly committed to equal rights for all, there must be federal legislation that applies across the country, public, and private sector alike. The hodgepodge of state legislation is not adequate, and the statement by President Obama that the federal government would no longer enforce Section 2 of the 14th Amendment is not enough. There must be clear direction and leadership. Without such, there is no equality of rights.

STOP DO NOT TURN THE PAGE UNTIL TOLD TO DO SO.
DO NOT RETURN TO A PREVIOUS TEST.

Chapter 7
Section 3: Science

• •

The Science section consists of multiple-choice, fill-in-the-blank, drop-down, drag-and-drop, hot-spot, and short-answer items intended to measure general concepts in science. The questions are based on short passages that may include a graph, chart, or figure. Study the information given and then answer the question(s) following it. Refer to the information as often as necessary in answering the questions, but remember that you have a time limit, and you should try to spend as little time on any item as you can and still get the correct answer.

You have 90 minutes to complete this section including answering a short-answer prompt, which should take about 10 minutes. The answers and explanations to this section's questions are in Chapter 9. Go through the explanations to all the questions, even for the ones you answered correctly. The explanations are a good review of the techniques we discuss throughout the book.

Unless you require accommodations, you'll be taking the GED test on a computer. Instead of marking your answers on a separate answer sheet, like you do for the practice test sections in this book, you'll see clickable ovals and fill-in-the-blank text boxes, and you'll be able to click with your mouse and drag and drop items where indicated. We formatted the questions and answer choices in this book to make them appear as similar as possible to what you'll see on the computer-based test, but we had to retain some A, B, C, D choices for marking your answers, and we provide an answer sheet for you to do so.

Answer Sheet for Section 3, Science

1.	(A) (B) (C) (D)			26.	(A) (B) (C) (D)		
2.	(A) (B) (C) (D)			27.	(A) (B) (C) (D)		
3.	(A) (B) (C) (D)			28.	(A) (B) (C) (D)		
4.	(A) (B) (C) (D)			29.	(A) (B) (C) (D)		
5.				30.	(A) (B) (C) (D)		
6.	(A) (B) (C) (D)			31.	(A) (B) (C) (D)		
7.				32.	(A) (B) (C) (D)		
8.	(A) (B) (C) (D)			33.	(A) (B) (C) (D)		
9.	(A) (B) (C) (D)			34.			
10.				35.			
11.				36.	(A) (B) (C)		
12.	(A) (B) (C) (D)			37.	(A) (B) (C) (D)		
13.	(A) (B) (C) (D)			38.	(A) (B) (C) (D)		
14.	(A) (B) (C) (D)			39.	(A) (B) (C) (D)		
15.	(A) (B) (C) (D)			40.	(A) (B) (C) (D)		
16.	(A) (B) (C) (D)			41.	(A) (B) (C) (D)		
17.	(A) (B) (C) (D)			42.			
18.	(A) (B) (C) (D)			43.			
19.	(A) (B) (C) (D)			44.	(A) (B) (C) (D)		
20.	(A) (B) (C) (D)			45.	(A) (B) (C) (D)		
21.				46.			
22.	(A) (B) (C) (D)			47.	(A) (B) (C)		
23.	(A) (B) (C) (D)			48.	(A) (B) (C) (D)		
24.	(A) (B) (C) (D)			49.	(A) (B) (C) (D)		
25.	(A) (B) (C) (D)			50.	(A) (B) (C) (D)		

Science Test

Time: 90 minutes

Directions: Read each item carefully and mark your answer on the answer sheet provided by filling in the corresponding oval or writing your answer in the blank box.

Questions 1–2 refer to the following passage.

Insulation

During the winter, you need something to keep warmth in the house and cold air out. In the summer, you need something to keep heat outside and cooler air inside. What you need is insulation.

Insulation reduces or prevents the transfer of heat (called *thermal transfer*) from the inside out or the outside in. Fiberglass and plastic foam provide such insulation because they contain trapped air. Normally, air is not a good insulator because the currents in air transfer the heat from one place to another. Trapping the air in small places, however, slows or prevents the transfer of heat. Think about these little packets of air the next time you sit in a warm house, safe from the frigid air of winter.

Joe J.J. Johnson, the world-famous architect and building supervisor, has developed a standard vacation home that he builds for his clients. This house has one floor-to-ceiling glass wall that overlooks the best feature of the client's lot. The other walls are cinder block covered with a cosmetic coat of concrete.

Mr. Johnson has been hired to build one of his famous designs for a client who lives in Juno, Alaska, in a huge home with a spectacular view of the Gastineau Channel. The client has requested a variation on the standard design to reduce his heating costs.

1. What variation would make the most sense to reduce the heating costs?

   (A) Have a floor-to-ceiling window facing away from the channel toward the front of the property.

   (B) Replace the floor-to-ceiling window with a cinder block wall.

   (C) Order curtains to cover the floor-to-ceiling window.

   (D) Order an oversized furnace.

2. What other ways could the homeowner consider to reduce the cost of energy to heat the house?

   (A) Add as much additional insulation as possible.

   (B) Use the house only during the summer months.

   (C) Wear clothing with thermal padding in the house.

   (D) All of the above.

Questions 3–5 refer to the following passage.

Metabolism

The process of metabolism is an essential process in every living cell. Metabolism allows the cell to obtain and distribute energy, which is necessary for survival. Light from the sun is absorbed and converted into chemical energy by photosynthesis, and it is this chemical energy that is necessary for animals to survive.

Go on to next page ⟹

One of the primary carbohydrates derived from plants is glucose. Through a process called *glycolysis,* energy is obtained from glucose. This reaction takes place in mitochondria, and the glucose molecule is broken down into pyruvic acids, which are further broken down into molecules, such as ethanol and lactic acid. This process is cyclical as the energy produced keeps the fermentation going.

Pyruvic acids are broken down to carbon dioxide and water by respiration, which releases far more energy. What started out as sunlight has become through photosynthesis the energy that keeps animals alive.

3. How do animals depend on plants to stay alive?

   (A) Animals need the shade provided by plants.

   (B) Cures for some diseases originate in plants.

   (C) Plants provide a comfortable environment for animals.

   (D) Plants provide animals with chemical potential energy.

4. What would happen to a plant if you covered it with a cloth that does not allow light to pass through it?

   (A) The plant would stop growing.

   (B) The leaves would shrivel.

   (C) The flower would fall off.

   (D) The plant would starve to death.

5. The chemical that is key to providing animals with energy is [   ].

Questions 6–7 refer to the following passage.

Velocity and Speed

There is a difference between speed and velocity, though sometimes you see the words used interchangeably. The *velocity* of a body is its rate of motion in a specific direction, such as a bicycle traveling 34 miles per hour due east. Because velocity has both magnitude (34 miles per hour) and direction (due east), it can be represented by a vector.

Speed has a magnitude only. If a bicycle travels at a speed of 28 miles per hour, you know its magnitude (28 miles per hour) but not its direction. Because speed has a magnitude but not a direction, it can be represented as a scalar.

6. If force is defined as that which is required to change the state or motion of an object in magnitude and direction, how should it be represented?

   (A) wavy lines

   (B) straight line

   (C) scalar

   (D) vector

7. A GPS is a device that shows you your position on Earth and can give you directions to get to another location on Earth. The directions given by a GPS are really in the form of [   ].

Go on to next page

Questions 8–9 refer to the following diagram, which is excerpted from Physical Science: What the Technology Professional Needs to Know, *by C. Lon Enloe, Elizabeth Garnett, Jonathan Miles, and Stephen Swanson (Wiley).*

Newcomen's Steam Engine

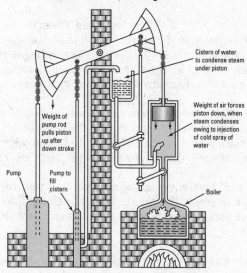

Cistern of water to condense steam under piston

Weight of air forces piston down, when steam condenses owing to injection of cold spray of water

Weight of pump rod pulls piston up after down stroke

Pump

Pump to fill cistern

Boiler

©John Wiley & Sons, Inc.

8. What properties of water and steam allow Newcomen's steam engine to operate?

   (A) Water is heavier than steam.

   (B) Steam condenses when cooled, occupying less space.

   (C) The boiler provides the energy to move the pump.

   (D) The pump rod is heavy enough to pull the arm down.

9. What effect does the condensation of steam in the cylinder with the piston have on the pump that fills the cistern?

   (A) It controls the fire in the boiler.

   (B) It pumps water from the cistern to the boiler.

   (C) It causes the pump to fill the cistern with water.

   (D) It forces the piston down.

Question 10 refers to the following figure.

The Food Chain

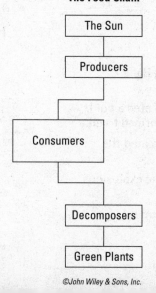

The Sun

Producers

Consumers

Decomposers

Green Plants

©John Wiley & Sons, Inc.

Go on to next page

10. If the number of consumers in an ecosystem began to multiply without control, the result to the balance of the ecosystem would be [   ].

Questions 11–14 refer to the following passage.

The Big Bang Theory

It is hard enough to imagine the universe as it is now and even harder to create a theory about how it all began. In the 1940s, George Gamow began to develop such a theory. Georges Lemaitre, another scientist, had also been working on the problem, and Gamow used some of the ideas of Lemaitre to develop his theory.

Gamow proposed the following theory: Somewhere between 10 and 21 billion years ago, there was a giant explosion in space. Before the explosion, the universe was the size of an atomic nucleus, with a temperature of about 10 billion degrees. The explosion started the expansion of the universe. Quarks, or elemental particles, existed in huge numbers.

Within a millisecond, the universe had expanded to the size of a grapefruit. The temperature cooled to 1 billion degrees. The quarks began to clump into protons and neutrons. Minutes later, the universe was still too hot for electrons and protons to form into atoms: a super-hot, fog-like environment.

With passing time and cooling temperatures, nuclear reactions took place, and within 300,000 years, atoms of hydrogen and helium began to emerge. As the atoms formed, light began to shine. The universe was taking shape.

Gravity began to act on the atoms and transform them into galaxies. Within 1 billion years of that first great explosion, galaxies and stars began to form. Within 15 billion years, planets began to emerge from the heavy elements thrown off by the dying of stars. The universe started with a big bang and continues to grow and change according to this theory.

11. The temperature of the first tiny particles was thought to be [   ] billion degrees.

12. For galaxies to have been transformed from atoms, what was necessary?

    (A) heat

    (B) pressure

    (C) centrifugal force

    (D) gravity

13. This theory is called the "Big Bang" because

    (A) An interplanetary war created a void, which the planets were formed to fill.

    (B) An immense explosion created the planets.

    (C) Hydrogen causes immense explosions when ignited.

    (D) The explosion was very loud.

14. How is the formation of hydrogen and helium atoms related to the possible destruction from an atomic bomb?

    (A) Both use hydrogen.

    (B) No relation exists.

    (C) Both result from explosions.

    (D) Both are nuclear reactions.

Go on to next page

Questions 15–17 refer to the following passage.

The Jellyfish

One of the creatures living in all the world's oceans is the jellyfish. Although it lives in the ocean, it is not a fish. The jellyfish is an invertebrate — that is, an animal lacking a backbone. Not only does it lack a backbone, but the jellyfish also has no heart, blood, brain, or gills and is more than 95 percent water.

Around the bell-like structure of the body, the jellyfish has *tentacles* — long tendrils that contain stinging cells — which are used to capture prey. The movement of the prey triggers the sensory hair in the stinging cell, and the prey is then in trouble.

Unfortunately, people are also in trouble if they get too close to the tentacles of a jellyfish. The stings are not fatal to humans but can cause a great deal of discomfort.

15. Why is a jellyfish classified as an invertebrate?

    (A) It has tentacles.

    (B) It has a small brain.

    (C) It has a primitive circulatory system.

    (D) It has no backbone.

16. What are the possible consequences for a swimmer swimming in the vicinity of a school of jellyfish?

    (A) They look weird.

    (B) Swimmers can get caught in the tentacles.

    (C) Swimmers may accidentally swallow a jellyfish.

    (D) The jellyfish may sting the swimmer, and the stings are painful.

17. Why do most small ocean creatures try to avoid jellyfish?

    (A) Jellyfish get in the way of the fish when they are feeding.

    (B) Jellyfish sting and eat small ocean creatures.

    (C) Fish are afraid of the strange-looking creatures.

    (D) Jellyfish and ocean creatures compete for the same food sources.

Questions 18–25 refer to the following passage.

Laws of Conservation

You are faced with laws every day. You cannot speed on the roads, and you cannot park wherever you choose.

Science has its laws as well. One such law is that energy cannot be created or destroyed. This law, called the law of conservation of energy, makes sense because you cannot create something from nothing. If you have an electrical charge, you cannot simply make it disappear.

A further law of conservation is the law of conservation of matter, which says that matter cannot be created or destroyed. This means that when a chemical change occurs, the total mass of an object remains constant. When you melt an ice cube, the water that results is neither heavier nor lighter than the original ice cube.

Go on to next page

18. Trees are damaged when struck by lightning, but the lightning is nowhere apparent afterward. Because lightning is a form of energy, what would explain the apparent disappearance of the energy in the lightning?

   (A) The energy in the lightning disappears.

   (B) The energy in the lightning must be conserved and is transformed into another form of energy that affects the tree.

   (C) The tree absorbs the lightning and stores the energy for future use.

   (D) Lightning striking the tree creates new energy, which damages the tree.

19. What is the purpose of laws in science?

   (A) Science is an ordered discipline, and the laws provide the requisite order.

   (B) Laws set parameters within which scientists can proceed with their investigations.

   (C) Laws make it easier to study science because they provide a logical order to the information studied.

   (D) All of the above.

20. When a magician makes a rabbit appear in a hat, it is an example of which law of science?

   (A) conservation of energy

   (B) conservation of matter

   (C) creation of illusion

   (D) conservation of resources

21. When an iceberg melts as a result of temperature changes, the law of science that is being best illustrated is [   ].

22. When you take a dead battery out of your flashlight, what has happened to its original charge?

   (A) It has been converted into light.

   (B) It has disappeared.

   (C) The battery has worn out.

   (D) The energy has been destroyed.

23. How would a scientist categorize the result of adding 3 ounces of water to 1 ounce of salt?

   (A) An example of the law of conservation of energy in that the amount of energy would be the same afterward as before.

   (B) You will end up with 1 ounce of salty water.

   (C) The salt will disappear, and all that will remain is water.

   (D) An example of the law of conservation of mass in that the total mass will remain the same.

24. A ball rolling down a hill cannot stop by itself. What law of science explains this?

   (A) There is a bump on the road.

   (B) The ball has no brakes.

   (C) The energy from rolling down the hill can't disappear.

   (D) The theory of the laws of conservation keeps the ball from stopping.

25. What is the purpose of laws in science?

   (A) They summarize the results of a group of experimental results in a form that can be understood and remembered.

   (B) They represent the sum of positive reproducible experimental results in a coherent summary statement.

   (C) They represent the mathematical or verbal summary of a series of diverse experimental results that may not otherwise be recognized as related.

   (D) All of the above.

Go on to next page

Questions 26–28 refer to the following passage.

Why Do Birds Fly South for the Winter?

Every fall, the sky is full of birds flying south for the winter. However, you can still see a few birds in the northern part of the country during the winter. Scientists have advanced theories about this phenomenon.

Some birds eat insects for food. In winter, many species of birds fly south, because that's where the food exists. In southern states, insects are available all year long, providing a banquet for the birds, whereas in the northern parts of the country, insects (as well as other food sources, such as seeds and berries) are scarce or even nonexistent during the winter. The birds fly south for winter to follow the food. In the spring, as insects once again become plentiful in the northern states, the birds still follow the food, this time to the north.

26. Why do migratory birds return to the northern states in the spring?

    (A) They miss their summer homes.

    (B) It gets too hot in the southern states.

    (C) They are able to find food again.

    (D) They fly north out of habit.

27. How is the population of insects in a geographical area related to the regular migratory pattern of birds?

    (A) Insects bite the birds.

    (B) The insects lead the birds south.

    (C) Some birds eat insects.

    (D) Birds have a habit of always eating the same insects.

28. Why are scientists interested in the migration of birds?

    (A) It happens regularly and apparently without reason.

    (B) Scientists like to go south.

    (C) Someone asked the scientists about it.

    (D) Scientists look for connections between caterpillars and travel.

Questions 29–30 refer to the following passage.

The Law of Unintended Consequences

Lake Victoria is the largest freshwater lake in Africa. It once had abundant fish, which provided protein for the local people who ate the fish. Unfortunately, a new species — the Nile Perch — was introduced into the lake by fishermen looking for a challenging fishing experience to attract their share of tourists interested in exploring the area.

The Nile Perch is an aggressive predator and had no natural enemies in Lake Victoria. It quickly ate up large numbers of the smaller fish, which affected the diets of the local population. These smaller fish ate algae and parasite-bearing snails. Without the smaller fish eating them, the live algae spread over the surface of the lake. Dead algae sank to the bottom of the lake and decayed, a process that consumed oxygen necessary for the fish living deep in the lake.

The snails, without natural predators, and the parasites they carried multiplied, creating a serious health hazard to the population. The introduction of a fish to encourage tourism had a detrimental effect on the lake and the population that depended on it.

Go on to next page

29. What human intervention caused the destruction of the ecological balance in Lake Victoria?

    (A) shrinking populations of snails

    (B) freshwater lake

    (C) growing populations of smaller fish

    (D) the Nile Perch

30. Why is it seldom beneficial to introduce a foreign species into a stable environment?

    (A) The foreign species has plenty of predators.

    (B) The other species in the lake would not have to compete for food.

    (C) The foreign species is bad for sport fishermen.

    (D) The foreign species can upset the ecological balance.

Questions 31–34 refer to the following table, which is adapted from Hands-On General Science Activities with Real-Life Applications, *by Pam Walker and Elaine Wood (Wiley).*

Space Travel

Characteristic	Moon	Mars
Distance from Earth	239,000 miles	48,600,000 miles
Gravity	$\frac{1}{6}$ Earth's gravity	$\frac{1}{3}$ Earth's gravity
Atmosphere	None	Thin carbon dioxide, 1% air pressure of Earth
Trip time	3 days	1.88 Earth years
Communication time	2.6 seconds, round trip	10 to 41 minutes, round trip

31. If you were an aeronautical engineer planning a journey to Mars, why would you prefer to go to a space station on the moon and then launch the rocket to Mars instead of going directly from Earth to Mars?

    (A) Lower gravity on the moon means you need less fuel for the launch.

    (B) You have more space to take off and land on the moon.

    (C) No atmosphere means an easier takeoff.

    (D) The moon is closer to Earth than Mars.

32. If you were a communications engineer trying to establish a safety network to warn a rocket ship of dangers, where would you place the transmitter for this rocket ship's journey to Mars?

    (A) on the moon

    (B) on Earth

    (C) on Mars

    (D) not enough information given

33. Why would a trip to the moon be a better first choice than a trip to Mars for space travelers?

    (A) You can see the moon from Earth without a telescope.

    (B) The time of the trip is much shorter.

    (C) The moon has a better atmosphere.

    (D) There are already space vehicles on the moon.

34. If you held a pole-vaulting contest on the moon and Mars, the same contestant would vault higher with the same expenditure of energy on ⬚⬚⬚⬚ .

Go on to next page ⟹

> *Questions 35–37 refer to the following passage.*

Heredity, Then and Now

How often have you seen a young child and said, "She takes after her parents"? Many traits in a child do come from her parents. Physical and other characteristics, such as hair color and nose shape, are transmitted from one generation to the next. These characteristics, passed from one generation to the next, exist because of genetic code.

The first scientist to experiment with heredity was Gregor Mendel during the 19th century. Mendel experimented with pea plants and noted that characteristics appearing in "child" plants were similar to the "parent" plants. Mendel hypothesized that these characteristics were carried from generation to generation by "factors." It took many years of research to understand why children often look like their parents, but genetic code is now the basis of the study of heredity.

35. According to the passage, ⬚⬚⬚⬚ is a primary determinant for characteristics of the next generation.

36. The factors that Mendel hypothesized carried traits from one generation to the next is

    (A) traits

    (B) protons

    (C) genetic code

37. If you want to grow monster-sized pumpkins, from what kind of pumpkins do you want to get seeds to increase the probability of growing larger-than-average pumpkins?

    (A) orange pumpkins

    (B) monster-sized pumpkins

    (C) larger-than-average pumpkins

    (D) healthy pumpkins

> *Questions 38–39 refer to the following passage.*

The Space Shuttle

NASA has designed and built six space shuttles: Atlantis, Challenger, Columbia, Discovery, Endeavor, and Enterprise. The space shuttles are made up of two distinct parts: the orbiter and the booster rocket. The booster rocket provides the additional thrust to get the space shuttle away from the gravitational pull of the earth. The orbiter carries the people and payload as well as the workings of the shuttle. In a space flight, the booster is jettisoned after clearing the earth's gravitational pull, and the orbiter continues on its way.

38. Why would the booster be jettisoned during flight?

    (A) because the shuttle needs to add weight

    (B) to increase the size of the shuttle

    (C) to make the shuttle less maneuverable for landing

    (D) because it is no longer needed

39. Which part of a shuttle carries the payload?

    (A) booster

    (B) cockpit

    (C) orbiter

    (D) rocket

Go on to next page

> *Questions 40–41 refer to the following figure, which is excerpted from* Physical Science:
> What the Technology Professional Needs to Know, *by C. Lon Enloe, Elizabeth Garnett,*
> *Jonathan Miles, and Stephen Swanson (Wiley).*

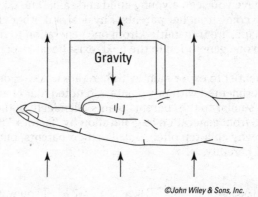

©John Wiley & Sons, Inc.

40. Work is defined as the product of force times displacement. Consider the diagram. If the force of gravity is greater than the forces being exerted by the muscles controlling the hand, what would happen?

(A) Nothing would happen.

(B) The hand would move downward.

(C) The hand would move to the right.

(D) The hand would move upward.

41. If an athlete knows that building muscles requires doing work against a weight, what would the athlete want to change in this diagram?

(A) Move the hand upward faster.

(B) Add weight to the hand.

(C) Close the fist as the arm is raised.

(D) Exhale as the arm is raised.

> *Questions 42–43 refer to the following passage, which is adapted from* The Sciences: An
> Integrated Approach, *3rd Edition, by James Trefil and Robert M. Hazen (Wiley).*

Copying DNA Sequence

The polymerase chain reaction (PCR) copies a sequence of DNA. To do this, a strand of DNA is mixed with nucleotides (DNA precursors). Nucleotides target a specific piece of DNA, as well as polymerase, an enzyme that helps to assemble DNA. Heat is applied until the temperature reaches 200°F. The energy from the heating separates the DNA strands. The mixture is then cooled to 140°F. At this temperature, the primers attach themselves to the DNA strands. Raising the temperature to 160°F causes the nucleotides to begin to attach to the DNA strands. After all this, two copies of the DNA are created.

Go on to next page

42. To separate the DNA strands during the polymerase chain reaction, the addition of ⬚ is necessary.

43. To clone an organism, you require an identical DNA blueprint. The PCR is something a scientist who is interested in cloning would want to study because ⬚.

Questions 44–45 refer to the following passage.

Dogs and Wolves — Relatives?

Current scientific theory is that the familiar family pet, the dog, descended from the wolf, but the dog has taken a very different path. The dog was the first animal to be domesticated, right around the end of the Ice Age.

Dogs are part of an extended family called *Canidae,* which contains 38 different species. Jackals, foxes, wolves, and dogs are all part of this family. Although they are related, wolves and dogs are different. Wolves have smaller heads for the same body weight. Dogs have smaller teeth, a more curved lower jaw, and eyes that are more rounded and forward looking. At a distance, however, many of these differences are difficult to spot.

44. What feature makes the wolf better adapted to hunting in the wild?

    (A) heavier coat

    (B) larger body

    (C) larger teeth

    (D) larger paws

45. What attribute of dogs makes them a better household pet than other members of the Canidae family?

    (A) There are many types of dogs to choose from.

    (B) Dogs were domesticated.

    (C) Dogs protect people's houses.

    (D) Dogs can help the visually impaired.

Questions 46–48 refer to the following passage.

Isotopes

Isotopes are chemical cousins. They are related to each other, but each isotope has slightly different — but related — atoms. Each of the related atoms has the same number of protons but a different number of neutrons. Because the number of electrons or protons determines the atomic number, isotopes have the same atomic number.

The number of neutrons determines the mass number. Because the number of neutrons in each isotope is different, the mass number is also different. These cousins all have different mass numbers but the same atomic number. Their chemical properties are similar but not the same. Like most cousins, they have family resemblances, but each has a unique personality.

Go on to next page

46. Different elements would have different numbers of ⬚.

47. Isotopes of a chemical have the same

    (A) number of neutrons

    (B) mass number

    (C) atomic number

48. A scientist has found related atoms in two different substances. If both atoms have the same atomic number but different mass numbers, what preliminary conclusion can be reached about the atoms?

    (A) They are the same substance.

    (B) They are isotopes.

    (C) They are different substances.

    (D) One is a compound of the other.

Questions 49–50 refer to the following passage.

How to Survive the Winter

When the temperature drops and the wind blows cold, you may think of animals that don't have homes to keep out the cold and worry about their ability to survive the winter. Not much food is available, temperatures in northern states go into the sub-zero range, and shelter is limited. How do they survive the winter?

Many animals can find shelter and hibernate for the winter. Hibernation is a sleeplike condition in which the animal's heartbeat, temperature, and metabolism slow down to adapt to the colder temperatures. This dormant condition prevents their starving or freezing during the harsh winters.

49. To survive the winter, bears do what?

    (A) Live in warm caves.

    (B) Grow heavy winter coat.

    (C) Absorb the sun's rays to keep warm.

    (D) Find a safe shelter and hibernate.

50. Why should you not disturb a hibernating animal?

    (A) It gets grouchy when awakened suddenly.

    (B) It could have trouble falling asleep again.

    (C) You should never bother a wild animal.

    (D) It would not be able to find enough food to survive.

Go on to next page

Short Answer

Passage

Everyone is familiar with cheddar cheese. People put it in sandwiches, on top of hamburgers, and eat it as a snack. People seem to like its orange color and slightly sharp taste, but what if they were served a slice of this common cheese with white specks on its surface? Then they might decide on another type of cheese for their next snack or sandwich. The local hamburger emporium may decide to substitute Swiss cheese for cheddar on its burgers to reduce complaints. These white spots present a problem.

The white spots are a substance called *calcium lactate crystals* and develop most often on the surfaces of naturally smoked cheddar cheese. Producers are very much aware of the problems caused by calcium lactate crystals as you can tell by the fact that naturally smoked cheddar cheese is more expensive than the everyday processed cheddar, and it's considered more of a gourmet item. Customers who pay more for what they believe is a better, more natural product do not appreciate white spots on the surface of their purchase. The other problem facing retailers and wholesalers of naturally smoked cheddar is that the amount of calcium lactate crystals increases with time and what may appear to be clear of the problem one day could look very different with the passage of time.

Food scientists have been studying these white spots because they cause a problem for sellers of this product. Scientists have investigated chemical changes that may or may not occur during natural smoking that could produce this unwanted substance. In order to proceed with this study, scientists took a large block of cheddar and cut out two equal and equivalent blocks of cheese. They smoked one block in a commercial smokehouse and stored the other without smoking. After two days, they analyzed the samples for moisture, lactate, pH, and water-soluble calcium.

The results proved to be interesting. The smoked sample contained significantly lower moisture and a lower pH level. There was a higher total lactate-in-moisture and water-soluble calcium-in-moisture level at the surface of the samples. After a period of ten weeks, there were some changes in the levels with the pH, total lactate-in-moisture and water-soluble calcium-in-moisture levels remaining constant. It was concluded that the smoking process predisposes the cheddar to surface calcium lactate crystal formation.

Prompt

Why would a scientist be interested in white specks on cheddar cheese and how did the results of the experiment help in solving the problem? Write your answer in the space provided. This task may require approximately 10 minutes to complete.

Chapter 8

Section 4: Mathematical Reasoning

The Mathematical Reasoning section consists of a series of questions intended to measure general mathematics skills and problem-solving ability. The questions are based on short readings that may include a graph, chart, or figure.

You have 90 minutes to complete this section. The answers and explanations to this section's questions are in Chapter 9. Go through the explanations to all the questions, even for the ones you answered correctly. The explanations are a good review of the mathematical techniques we discuss throughout the book.

Formulas you may need are given on the page before the first test question. Only some of the questions require you to use a formula, and you may not need all the formulas given. *Note:* If you can memorize the formulas and understand how to use them, you'll save a bit of time on the test, and then you can use that time saved for review or for harder items that you may have more trouble with.

Unless you require accommodations, you'll be taking the GED test on a computer. Instead of marking your answers on a separate answer sheet, like you do for the practice test sections in this book, you'll see clickable ovals and fill-in-the-blank text boxes, and you'll be able to click with your mouse and drag and drop items where indicated. We formatted the question and answer choices in this book to make them appear as similar as possible to what you'll see on the computer-based test, but we had to retain some A, B, C, D choices for marking your answers, and we provide an answer sheet for you to do so.

Answer Sheet for Section 4, Mathematical Reasoning

1. Ⓐ Ⓑ Ⓒ Ⓓ
2. Ⓐ Ⓑ Ⓒ Ⓓ
3. _____
4. Ⓐ Ⓑ Ⓒ Ⓓ
5. _____
6. Ⓐ Ⓑ Ⓒ Ⓓ
7. Ⓐ Ⓑ Ⓒ Ⓓ
8. _____
9. Ⓐ Ⓑ Ⓒ Ⓓ
10. Ⓐ Ⓑ Ⓒ Ⓓ
11. _____
12. [grid]
13. Ⓐ Ⓑ Ⓒ Ⓓ
14. Ⓐ Ⓑ Ⓒ Ⓓ
15. Ⓐ Ⓑ Ⓒ Ⓓ
16. _____
17. [grid]
18. Ⓐ Ⓑ Ⓒ Ⓓ
19. Ⓐ Ⓑ Ⓒ Ⓓ
20. Ⓐ Ⓑ Ⓒ Ⓓ
21. Ⓐ Ⓑ Ⓒ Ⓓ
22. Ⓐ Ⓑ Ⓒ Ⓓ
23. Ⓐ Ⓑ Ⓒ Ⓓ

24. Ⓐ Ⓑ Ⓒ Ⓓ
25. _____
26. _____
27. Ⓐ Ⓑ Ⓒ Ⓓ
28. _____
29. _____
30. Ⓐ Ⓑ Ⓒ Ⓓ
31. _____
32. _____
33. Ⓐ Ⓑ Ⓒ Ⓓ
34. Ⓐ Ⓑ Ⓒ Ⓓ
35. Ⓐ Ⓑ Ⓒ Ⓓ
36. _____
37. Ⓐ Ⓑ Ⓒ Ⓓ
38. _____
39. Ⓐ Ⓑ Ⓒ Ⓓ
40. Ⓐ Ⓑ Ⓒ Ⓓ
41. [grid]
42. Ⓐ Ⓑ Ⓒ Ⓓ
43. Ⓐ Ⓑ Ⓒ Ⓓ
44. Ⓐ Ⓑ Ⓒ Ⓓ
45. _____
46. Ⓐ Ⓑ Ⓒ Ⓓ
47. Ⓐ Ⓑ Ⓒ Ⓓ
48. Ⓐ Ⓑ Ⓒ Ⓓ
49. Ⓐ Ⓑ Ⓒ Ⓓ
50. Ⓐ Ⓑ Ⓒ Ⓓ

Mathematics Formula Sheet

Area of a:

parallelogram

$A = bh$

trapezoid

$A = \frac{1}{2}h(b_1 + b_2)$

Surface Area and Volume of a:

rectangular/right prism	$SA = ph + 2B$	$V = Bh$
cylinder	$SA = 2\pi rh + 2\pi r^2$	$V = \pi r^2 h$
pyramid	$SA = \frac{1}{2}ps + B$	$V = \frac{1}{3}Bh$
cone	$SA = \pi rs + \pi r^2$	$V = \frac{1}{3}\pi r^2 h$
sphere	$SA = 4\pi r^2$	$V = \frac{4}{3}\pi r^3$

(p = perimeter of base B; $\pi \approx 3.14$)

Algebre

slope of a line

$m = \frac{y_2 - y_1}{x_2 - x_1}$

slope-intercept form
of the equation of a line

$y = mx + b$

point-slope form of the
equation of a line

$y - y_1 = m(x - x_1)$

standard form of a
quadratic equation

$y = ax^2 + bx + c$

quadratic formula

$x = \frac{-b \pm \sqrt{b^2 - 4ac}}{2a}$

Pythagorean theorem

$a^2 + b^2 = c^2$

simple interest

$I = prt$

(I = interest, p = principal, r = rate, t = time)

Mathematical Reasoning Test

Time: 90 minutes

Directions: Choose the appropriate answer for each question. Mark your answers on the answer sheet provided by filling in the corresponding oval, writing your answer in the blank box or marking your answer on the graph.

1. Dharma is making sale signs for the Super Summer Sale at the Super Saver Swim Shop. Sales tax in Dharma's state is 5%. She makes a series of signs:

    Sign A: ½ off all merchandise

    Sign B: Buy one item, get the second item of equal value free

    Sign C: 50% off all merchandise

    Sign D: Nine times your sales tax back

    What would a shrewd consumer notice about the signs?

    (A) Sign A offers a better buy.

    (B) Sign C offers the worst deal.

    (C) Sign D offers the worst deal.

    (D) Sign B offers a better deal.

2. Daryl is framing a picture. He draws the following diagram to help him make it:

    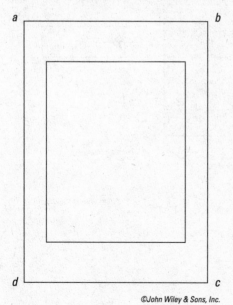

    ©John Wiley & Sons, Inc.

    Which of the following is true about the diagram?

    (A) *ab* must be perpendicular to *ad*.

    (B) *ab* must be parallel to *bc*.

    (C) *ad* must be parallel to *ab*.

    (D) *ab* and *dc* must be perpendicular.

3. The Hammerhill family is building a deck behind their house. The deck is to be 16 feet long and 21 feet wide, and the decking material was priced at $45.00 a square yard. The cost, in dollars, of the decking material would be [   ].

4. Margaret Millsford, the Chief Financial Officer of Aggravated Manufacturing Corporation, has to report to the Board of Directors. She has been instructed to analyze the sales of each of the company's product lines and recommend dropping the least profitable line. She found that although the per-unit profits of grommets and gadgets were the same, producing widgets off-shore doubled the profit. She prepared the following graph to demonstrate the relative volumes and made an oral presentation to illustrate the differing profitability of off-shore production and to back up her recommendation:

    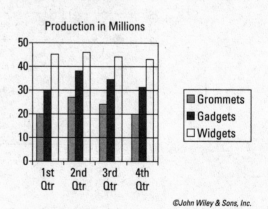

    ©John Wiley & Sons, Inc.

    Based on the graph and Margaret's oral presentation, her recommendation would be to drop

    (A) widgets

    (B) grommets

    (C) gadgets

    (D) grommets and widgets

Go on to next page

5. Quan is obsessive about his marks and how they compare to the rest of his class. On Quan's final report, his results were as follows:

Computer Studies: 97

English: 98

Mathematics: 99

Physical Education: 87

Science: 97

Social Studies: 94

Spanish: 86

The results for Quan's entire class were

Average: 93.27

Median: 96

Mode: 97

Range: 14

Calculate Quan's average, median, mode, and range, and then compare them to the results of his class. If Quan is most concerned about being admitted to college, the measure he should be most concerned about is [   ].

6. Alice was trying to explain how the length of time she could run each morning had improved each month since she started, except for the month she twisted her ankle. She drew the following graph to show her friends Mary and Kevin the average length of time (in minutes) she ran each day each month:

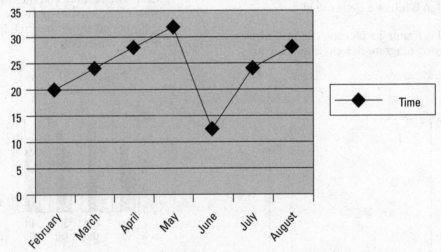

©John Wiley & Sons, Inc.

In which month did Alice likely twist her ankle?

(A) June

(B) February

(C) August

(D) September

Go on to next page

7. Dominic and Paula were comparing their report cards, as follows:

Dominic's Report Card

Subject	Grade (%)
Mathematics	63
Social Studies	76
Science	65
Language Arts	84
Physical Education	72

Paula's Report Card

Subject	Grade (%)
Mathematics	80
Social Studies	64
Science	76
Language Arts	72
Physical Education	88

The teacher told them that the ratio of their total marks was very close. What is the ratio of Paula's marks to Dominic's marks on these report cards?

(A) 9:10

(B) 18:19

(C) 10:9

(D) 19:18

8. In the series, 4, 6, 10, 18, . . . , the first term that is a multiple of 11 is [_____].

9. Simone follows the stock market very carefully. She has been following Cowardly Corporation the last few months, keeping track of her research in the following table:

Date	Closing Price (In U.S. Dollars)
August 7	15.03
August 17	16.12
September 1	14.83
September 9	15.01
September 16	14.94
September 20	15.06
September 23	15.17
September 24	15.19

Simone bought shares of the stock on September 24 and wants to make money before selling it. She paid 3% commission to her broker for buying and will pay the same again for selling. What is the lowest price (in U.S. dollars) for which Simone can sell each of her shares to break even?

(A) $16.48

(B) $16.13

(C) $15.66

(D) $20.00

10. If $22.4 = \dfrac{56a}{5a+10}$, what is the value of a?

(A) 0

(B) –56

(C) 4

(D) –4

Go on to next page

Questions 11–12 refer to the following graph.

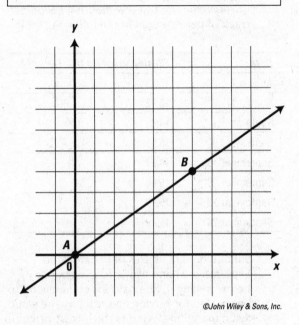

©John Wiley & Sons, Inc.

11. Calculate the slope of the line *AB*. The slope of *AB* is [＿＿＿＿＿].

12. If the slope of *AB* remains the same, but it intercepts the *y*-axis at *C* (0, 4), where does it intersect the *x*-axis? Use the graph on the answer sheet to indicate the point where *AB* intersects the *x*-axis.

13. If a fire is built in the center of a square barbeque pit, where is the safest place to stand to avoid the intense heat of the fire?

    (A) at a corner

    (B) along the left side

    (C) along the right side

    (D) not enough information given

14. Lydia and Wayne are shopping for carpets for their home and are looking for the best carpet at the best price. Carnie's Carpets offers them a wool carpet for $21.50 per square yard. Flora's Flooring says they will match that same carpet for only $2.45 per square foot, while Dora's Deep Discount offers them an 8-x-12-foot rug of the same carpet material for $210.24. What is the lowest price per square foot offered to Lydia and Wayne?

    (A) $2.45

    (B) $21.90

    (C) $2.19

    (D) $2.39

15. Miscellaneous Appliances Limited is concerned about its output at Plant A. For its annual report, company officials prepared the following graphs to show the output for each quarter of the last two years:

Output at Plant A – 2013

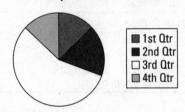

Output at Plant A – 2014

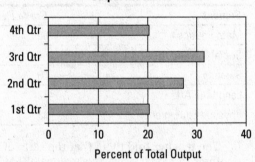

©John Wiley & Sons, Inc.

Which quarter showed a dramatic increase in production in 2014?

(A) third quarter

(B) first quarter

(C) fourth quarter

(D) second quarter

16. Mr. and Mrs. Ngs are looking to expand their two-story house and have calculated that they need at least another 630 square feet to live comfortably. They want to use the basement level for storage and the rest for living. A contractor quotes them $15.80 per square foot for the renovation without redecoration. A real estate agent tells them that they can increase the value of their home by about $18,000 by building the addition. If they want to add as much additional space as possible for the $18,000 they will recover, they would have to add [＿＿＿＿＿] additional square feet.

Go on to next page ⟹

17. An experiment involving throws of a 20-sided die produced the following results:

Throw	Left-Handed	Right-Handed
1	2	4
2	4	12
3	5	2
4	9	6
5	11	13
6	10	15
7	4	17
8	6	3
9	7	5

Use the graph on the answer sheet to indicate the point that represents the combined medians of the throws, using the median of the left-handed results as the *x*-value and the median of the right-handed results as the *y*-value.

18. LeeAnne is shopping for a new vehicle. She drives about 18,000 miles per year. She is most concerned about the cost of gasoline. She expects gasoline to average $3.50 a gallon during the five years she will own the car and is basing her decision on that price. As she shops, she creates a chart based on her calculations:

Type of Vehicle	Miles per Gallon
SUV	12.8
Sedan	19.6
2-door	19.5
All-wheel drive	17.2
Sports car	18.6

Based on her criteria, which car should LeeAnne buy?

(A) SUV

(B) sedan

(C) 2-door

(D) sports car

19. Tom is worried about getting to the GED testing center on time. He knows that he averages 40 miles per hour on the route to the test. If the test site is 47 miles from Tom's house and he wants to arrive 20 minutes early, how do you figure out how much time he needs to leave for travel and waiting?

(A) add then divide

(B) multiply then add

(C) divide then add

(D) add then multiply

20. Leonora has just received her mid-term report card. Her grades are as follows:

Leonora's Report Card

Subject	Grade (%)
English	84
Geography	78
Mathematics	68
Physical Education	77
Physics	82

Her average grade is 77.8%. To get into the college of her choice, she needs an average of 80%. English is her best subject. By how many percentage points will her English score have to go up, assuming all her other subjects stay the same, to get into college?

(A) 8

(B) 9

(C) 10

(D) 11

Go on to next page

21. Sonia has an amazing recipe for rice. For each 1 cup of rice, she adds 2 cups of vegetable soup and a quarter cup of lentils. This weekend, Sonia is having a large dinner party and figures she needs to cook 3½ cups of rice for her guests. How much of the other two ingredients should she use?

    (A) 7 cups of soup and ⅞ cup of lentils

    (B) 3½ cups of soup and ½ cup of lentils

    (C) 7 cups of soup and 1 cup of lentils

    (D) 1 cup of soup and 7 cups of lentils

22. In drawing cards from a deck, any single card has an equal chance of being drawn. After six cards have been drawn and removed, what is the probability of drawing an ace of hearts if it has not yet been drawn?

    (A) 1:50

    (B) 1:48

    (C) 1:46

    (D) 1:44

23. The Symons are redecorating a room in their house. They have some interesting ideas. They want to put a rug on the floor surrounded by a border of tiles. They are considering teak paneling halfway up each wall. In addition, they may cut away part of the ceiling to put in a skylight. This is a diagram of their room:

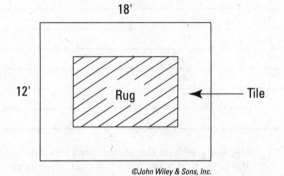

©John Wiley & Sons, Inc.

The rug costs $7.50 a square foot, and tile costs $9.00 a square foot. One rug they like is 16 feet by 10 feet, leaving just a little area around the rug for tiles. At the store, however, they see another rug that is only 12 feet by 8 feet, but it's just the right pattern and colors for their room. Which floor treatment is less expensive?

    (A) both are the same cost

    (B) the larger rug

    (C) the smaller rug without the paneling

    (D) the smaller rug

24. Brad is a secret shopper for the Friendly Furniture store. His job is to go to competitive stores and price a series of items to make sure his employer can advertise that he has the best prices. His boss wants to start a new advertising campaign: "Friendly Furniture — always lower than the average price of our competitors." Brad's job is to shop several stores to make sure the claim is accurate. Brad's results are recorded in the following table:

Item	Store A	Store B	Store C	Store D	Friendly Furniture
Couch	$1,729	$1,749	$1,729	$1,699	$1,719
Dining room set	$4,999	$4,899	$5,019	$4,829	$4,899
Loveseat	$1,259	$1,199	$1,279	$1,149	$1,229
Coffee table	$459	$449	$479	$429	$449
Reclining chair	$759	$799	$739	$699	$739

Which item cannot be advertised as "lower than the average price"?

(A) couch

(B) dining room set

(C) loveseat

(D) coffee table

Go on to next page

25. In a pistachio-eating contest, Sarah eats 48 pistachios in 18 minutes. If she could maintain her rate of eating pistachios, she could eat [_____] pistachios in 2 hours.

26. Kevin wants to paint his room, which is 9 feet 5 inches long, 8 feet 3 inches wide, and 8 feet 2 inches high. The paint can label cautions that air must be exchanged in the room every 12 minutes. When Kevin looks for exhaust fans to keep the air moving, he finds that they are calibrated in cubic feet per minutes. The operation that Kevin has to perform first to figure out which size fan he needs is [_____].

27. Which of these shapes has the same relationship to the horizontal after a 90-degree rotation about a point on the perimeter?

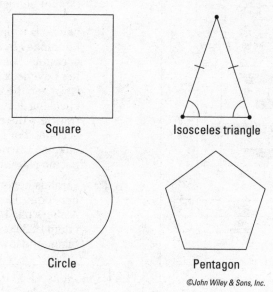

Square   Isosceles triangle

Circle   Pentagon

©John Wiley & Sons, Inc.

(A) isosceles triangle

(B) circle

(C) pentagon

(D) not enough information given

28. In a large company, the top four positions are organized as follows:

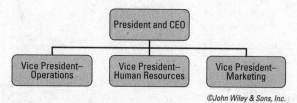

©John Wiley & Sons, Inc.

Each department has the following budget:

Department	Budget ($ Millions)
Operations	14.7
Human Resources	2.1
Marketing	5.6

What is the ratio of the largest budget to the smallest budget? [_____]

Go on to next page

29. A company has doubled its sales from the first to the third quarters. Graph ☐ indicates this pattern.

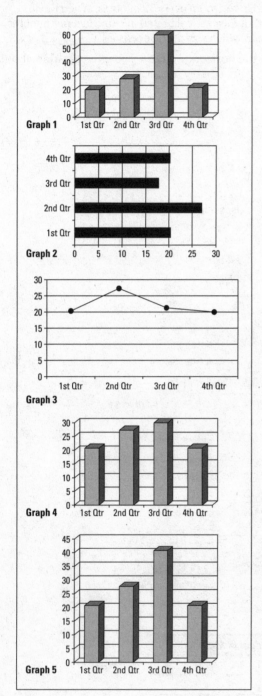

Graph 1

Graph 2

Graph 3

Graph 4

Graph 5

©John Wiley & Sons, Inc.

30. A 6-foot tall forester standing some 16 feet from a tree uses his digital rangefinder to calculate the distance between his eye and the top of the tree to be 25 feet. How tall is the tree?

(A) $\sqrt{41}$

(B) $\sqrt{881}$

(C) $\sqrt{256}$

(D) not enough information

31. Lawrie is trying to save money, so she keeps her money in both checking and savings accounts. Each week, she puts $24.00 from her paycheck into her savings account. However, the fourth week, she overdraws her checking account by $7.50, and the bank transfers the money from her savings account. For providing this service, the bank charges Lawrie $10.00. Her savings account balance after the fourth week is $☐.

32. Sarah is negotiating the price of a chair for her room. The original price was $96.00. Store A offers her 1/3 off. Store B offers her a discount of 30%. She will save $☐ by taking the lower price.

Questions 33–34 are based on the following information and figure.

While a rock band is setting up for a concert, the audio engineer is calibrating the amplifiers used for the concert. He has an instrument that develops and displays a graph for each setting on the amplifier controls. The graph appears like this:

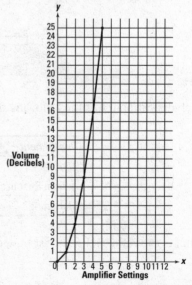

©John Wiley & Sons, Inc.

Go on to next page ➡

33. From the graph, calculate the volume in decibels for a setting of 10 on the amplifier.

    (A) 20

    (B) 30

    (C) 50

    (D) 100

34. The equation that produced this graph is $V = S^2$, where V is the volume in decibels and S is the volume setting. If the volume is 144, what is the volume setting on the amplifier?

    (A) 9

    (B) 10

    (C) 11

    (D) 12

35. In this particular auditorium, the volume of sound decreases by half for every 10 feet away from the stage a person sits. If the volume at the stage is 144 decibels, the volume in decibels for a person sitting 20 feet from the stage will be

    (A) 36

    (B) 48

    (C) 60

    (D) 72

36. Gary and Georgina George bought a new car and are trying to estimate the gas mileage. The new car travels 240 miles at a cost of $54.00. The price of gasoline is $2.70 per gallon. They estimate that the car will get 18 miles per gallon. The actual mileage would be [＿＿＿＿] miles per gallon.

Question 37 is based on the following figures, which are reprinted from Physical Science: What the Technology Professional Needs to Know, *by C. Lon Enloe, Elizabeth Garnett, Jonathan Miles, and Stephen Swanson (Wiley).*

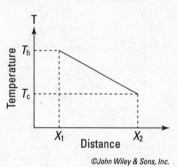

©John Wiley & Sons, Inc.

37. If the person pictured wants to remain at a constant temperature, what geometrical shape should he follow as a path?

    (A) ellipse

    (B) line

    (C) square

    (D) circle

Go on to next page

38. Igor is in charge of the swimming pool at the local recreation center. The pool is 120 feet long and 24 feet wide and holds 12,902 cubic feet of water. The average depth of the pool in feet is [   ].

Questions 39–42 refer to the following table.

Average Mileage and Annual Fuel Cost of Selected Vehicles

Vehicle	Mileage (Miles per Gallon) City	Mileage (Miles per Gallon) Highway	Annual Cost ($)*
A	23	28	840
B	21	29	875
C	19	25	1,000
D	18	24	1,050
E	17	22	1,105
F	16	22	1,167
G	15	21	1,235
H	14	19	1,314
I	13	18	1,400
J	12	16	1,823

*Annual cost includes 15,000 miles driven annually; 55% of the miles in the city and 45% on the highway; standard price of fuel

39. If you were in the market for a car, how much could you save, in dollars, over a three-year period, by buying the most economical car over the least economical car?

(A) 983

(B) 2,520

(C) 5,469

(D) 2,949

40. What is the difference in miles per gallon between the mean city mileage and the median of the city mileages for these vehicles?

(A) 1 2/3

(B) 1/3

(C) 17

(D) 2 1/2

Go on to next page

41. Use the graph on the answer sheet to indicate the results for Vehicle A with the difference between city and highway mileage as the appropriate point on the y-axis.

42. To solve a problem in her mathematics class, Jan had to solve the following set of equations:

    $2x + 3y = 10$

    $5x + 6y = 13$

    What is the correct value of y?

    (A) −8

    (B) −6

    (C) +6

    (D) +8

43. An international survey found the following information about participation in adult education:

Percent of Population over Age 21 Participating in Adult Education in the Year 2003

Country	Tocal Participation Rate (%)
Denmark	62.3
Hungary	17.9
Norway	43.1
Portugal	15.5
United States	66.4

Compare the participation rates of the countries with the highest and lowest participation rates by calculating approximately how many more adults participate in adult education in the country with the highest participation rate than in the country with the lowest participation rate.

(A) 2 times as many

(B) 4 times as many

(C) 6 times as many

(D) 8 times as many

Go on to next page

44. Gordon has the following six bills to pay this month:

Bill Payable To	Amount
Bedding by Vidalia	$23.00
Chargealot Credit Corp.	$31.00
Dink's Department Store	$48.00
Furniture Fit for a Princess Shoppe	$13.00
Highest Fidelity Sound Shop	$114.00
Overpriced Gas Corporation	$39.00

Each month, he allocates $250.00 to pay his bills. This month, his bills are over this budget. How much extra money must he find from other parts of his budget to pay all his bills?

(A) $8.00

(B) $268.00

(C) $28.00

(D) $18.00

45. Georgette needs $185 to buy books for her Geography course, but because her hours at work have been cut back this month, she cannot afford to buy them, even though she needs them. Walking to class, she notices a sign offering to loan her $200 for one month for $20 interest. She calculates that if she can repay the money within the month by working extra hours, she will be able to afford the principal and the interest.

When Georgette applies for the loan, she reads the contract carefully and notices that after the initial one-month period, the interest rate climbs to 15% per month and includes the previous month's principal and interest. If she earns $11.00 per hour, how many extra hours (to the nearest hour) would she have to work to pay the additional second month's interest? ☐

46. Andrew just bought a small circular swimming pool for his children. The diameter of the pool is 12 feet, and Andrew can fill it safely to a depth of 9 inches. If a cubic foot of water weighs 62.42 pounds, how many pounds does the water in Andrew's pool weigh?

(A) approximately 27,000

(B) approximately 2,700

(C) approximately 1,300

(D) approximately 5,300

47. If Giorgio borrows $100 for one year and three months and repays $108 including simple interest, what rate of interest was he charged?

(A) 6.4%

(B) 8.0%

(C) 4.0%

(D) 4.6%

48. Chico went shopping for some groceries for his family. His shopping list was as follows:

- 2 pounds of apples
- 5 bananas
- 1 container of milk
- 1 loaf of bread

If apples were $0.79 a pound, bananas $0.23 each, milk $1.27 a carton, and bread $0.98 a loaf, what is the approximate total cost of the groceries?

(A) $3.90

(B) $4.10

(C) $4.90

(D) $5.50

Go on to next page

49. From the numbers listed, what number should go in the box?

    SERIES, 4, 7, 12, 19, ☐, 38, ...

    (A) 28

    (B) 26

    (C) 24

    (D) 22

50. A rectangle 5 units long and 4 units high is represented on a graph. If three of the corners are placed at (3, 2), (3, –2), and (–2, 2), where should the fourth corner be placed?

    (A) (–2, 2)

    (B) (2, –2)

    (C) (–2, –2)

    (D) (2, 2)

STOP DO NOT TURN THE PAGE UNTIL TOLD TO DO SO.
DO NOT RETURN TO A PREVIOUS TEST.

Chapter 9
Answers and Explanations

Congratulations! Now that you've completed one or all of the sample test sections in Chapters 5 through 8, you can see how you did. In this chapter, we provide the answers and explanations to every question in the test sections. If you just want a quick look at the answers, check out the abbreviated answer key at the end of this chapter. However, if you have the time, be sure to read the answer explanations to help you understand why some answers were correct and others not, especially when the choices were really close. Remember, you learn as much from your errors as from the correct answers. Review these explanations as part of your overall learning process.

Note: This chapter doesn't contain sample answers for the Extended Response or short answer items. Refer to the relevant chapters for additional help on writing and evaluating your responses.

Answers for Section 1, Reasoning Through Language Arts

1. **B. a center housing social enterprises.** The column specifically states that the center houses 85 social enterprises. Choice (A) is totally wrong and can be instantly eliminated on first reading. The other answers have a ring of correctness because the column is about social enterprises, charities, and school leavers, but they have nothing to do with the center and, thus, are wrong.

2. **C. innovative programs.** The column states that the Learnxs Foundation supports innovative programs. All the other answers except for Choice (A) are mentioned or implied in the column; however, they aren't correct answers to the question. You have to read carefully and double-check the facts. Just because something is mentioned or is familiar doesn't mean it's the right answer to the question.

3. **distributing discarded materials to visual arts classes.** The passage clearly spells out that Artsjunction's function is to distribute discarded materials to visual arts classes.

4. **B. provide training in word and numerical processing to employees and clients.** The column is very specific about the purpose of the Microtron bus. It provided services to employees and clients of small businesses in word and numerical processing. The other answers sound like they could be right, but, after rereading the column, you can see that they aren't.

   When you're trying to answer these questions under time constraints, try to remember exactly what the passage said. If you only think you remember, go back as quickly as you can and skim the piece for key words. In this case, the key word is *Microtron*. It sometimes helps to read the question first before reading the passage.

5. **D. as a business incubator.** The passage very precisely spells out the mandate of the Training Renewal Foundation: to serve disadvantaged youth and displaced workers. Choices (A) and (B) may be worthy activities for any charity, but they aren't stated as part of the mandate and, thus, are wrong as answers. Choice (C) is just wrong and is a play on another meaning of *serves*. You can immediately exclude this answer and have only three others to consider.

6. **C. The employee must wear appropriate clothing.** Employees should wear appropriate clothing to project a professional appearance and maintain safety standards. The other requirements — such as refraining from alcohol use, not associating with paraphernalia, being respectful, and using non-offensive language — don't relate to appearance.

7. **A. Accept authority.** Employees must accept the authority of supervisors, as is stated clearly in the passage. The other choices may be partially correct, but they are not the best answer.

8. **D. personal conduct.** Employees must conduct themselves professionally so that the business grows and improves.

9. **B. by not inviting others in.** To ensure safety and security, employees shouldn't invite other people in. The promotion of dignity, interaction, and supervisors' meetings don't directly relate to ensuring safety and security.

10. **D. You are fired.** Repeated instances of noncompliance lead to dismissal. The other options aren't backed up by the passage.

11. **A. insert *and opportunities* between *challenges* and *never*.** Although the word *both* refers to two options, here, you're given only one option — *challenges*. If you insert *and opportunities* between *challenges* and *never*, you include a second option and correct the sentence.

12. **C. change *who* to *that*.** An organization is never a *who;* only people can be referred to as *who*. An organization is a collective noun made up of people, but the collective noun itself is an impersonal entity and doesn't qualify as a *who*.

    Although the sentence may appear long and, therefore, may benefit from rewriting, the sentence isn't technically incorrect. Although commas do serve to make sentences clearer, you don't want to insert them unless punctuation rules make them correct.

13. **B. has been working.** CanLearn Study Tours is a single entity because it's one company. Therefore, it's a singular noun and needs the singular verb *has* rather than the plural *have*.

    A company is always an *it*. Even though a company is made up of a lot of people, it's still a singular entity.

14. **B. change the comma after *following* to a colon.** You need to insert a colon before the list to introduce it.

15. **D. no correction required.** The options presented either make the sentence difficult to understand or introduce errors, so the correct answer is *no correction required*.

16. **A. change *organizations'* to *organizations*.** A stray apostrophe has landed on this sentence. The one after *organizations'* is unnecessary because you're not trying to show possession here. Choice (B) is incorrect, because the passage doesn't refer to *all* organizations. Choice (C) would introduce a homonym error, and Choice (D) inserts the wrong tense.

    Get comfortable with the uses of apostrophes — especially those used for possession — before taking the GED Reasoning Through Language Arts test.

17. **B. discover a new source of revenue in these.** You need to correct the spelling error by changing *soarce* to *source*.

18. **C. change *formats* to *format*.** *Formats* is plural, but *has* is a singular verb. Verbs and their subjects must agree. There is no need for a comma after seminar or an apostrophe after sales. The apostrophe would indicate ownership, which isn't the case here. A period after *seminars* would create two sentence fragments, also an error.

    Study both subject-verb agreement and pronoun-antecedent agreement before taking the Reasoning Through Language Arts test.

19. **B. replace *insured* with *ensured*.** Choice(B) corrects the spelling error by changing *insured* to *ensured*.

    Using *insure* is a common error. Use *insure* only when you mean the service you buy to protect your car, house, health, life, and so on. This example has nothing to do with insurance, so use *ensure* instead.

20. **D. no correction required.** The other choices don't improve or correct the sentence.

21. **B. Journey up the Hudson.** To get to the Kaatskill Mountains, you need to journey up the Hudson. A dismembered branch and fresh green aren't locations that can better help you locate the mountains. Although asking directions may work, this approach isn't mentioned in the passage.

22. **D. with magical hues and shapes.** The wives use the magical hues and shapes of the mountains to forecast the weather. Other factors, such as the evening sky or gray vapors aren't as good of indicators. A barometer is an instrument to measure air pressure.

23. **C. light smoke curling.** To help you locate the village, you first need to look for light smoke curling from chimneys. You can't see the other sign, shingle-roofs, until after you can see the smoke. Blue tints aren't signs for locating villages.

24. **Dutch colonists.** The Dutch colonists were the newcomers who founded the village. Although there are others named, they're the incorrect answer. Peter Stuyvesant established the government. The great Appalachian family refers to the mountains.

25. **A. He has since died.** Peter Stuyvesant, who had headed the government, had since died. The other answer choices describe Stuyvesant as an original settler, a soldier, and a governor, but they don't refer to his death.

26. **yellow bricks.** Settlers brought yellow bricks from Holland to build the houses. Other materials, such as weather-cocks, windows, and shingle-roofs, were acquired locally.

27. **Hawkins's fields.** Dave worked as a field hand on Hawkins's farm. He hopes his mother will let him buy a gun with his wages from Hawkins.

28. **A. show he wasn't "scareda" the others.** He wants to show the other field hands that he isn't scared of them. Dave mentions that he isn't afraid of them just before he first discusses buying the gun.

29. **D. from the Sears-Roebuck "catlog."** Dave had to purchase the gun through the Sears-Roebuck catalog. Joe didn't keep guns in his store. Neither Mr. Hawkins nor Ma are sources of guns.

30. **B. by a yellow lantern glow.** Joe kept a yellow lantern glowing on the porch. Other answer choices, such as *the smell of mackerel, the banging screen door,* or *the coal oil smell* may also help you find the store, but they aren't the best indicators.

31. **A. He lost his nerve.** Dave lost his nerve and was afraid to ask Joe to see guns in the catalog. The other possibilities — it was too dark, he needed to get home for supper, or he made his own money — aren't the best answers.

32. **B. Convince Ma to give him the money.** Dave would have to convince Ma to give him the money to buy the gun. The other reasons, including finding it in the catalog, persuading Joe, or getting ol man Hawkins's permission, either aren't relevant or aren't as important as convincing Ma to give him the money.

33. **D. you to listen to each customer's assessment.** The *assessment* belongs to each customer and requires a possessive form of customer: *customer's.* The other answers are neither correct nor do they improve the sentence. Because customer is singular, you must insert the apostrophe before the *s* in *customer.*

34. **A. when she explains the situation from her perspective.** The meaning of this sentence is that the clerk should listen to the customer, so put the most important information first. The best way to start this sentence is with the *when she explains the situation from her perspective* phrase.

35. **C. change *waving* to *waiving*.** *Waving* means to motion with the hand, while *waive* means to dismiss. It may be interesting to wave at a charge, but the proper meaning of the sentence is to dismiss (or not collect) the charge. These two words are *homonyms* (words that sound the same but have different spellings and meanings). You are expected to understand most homonyms for this test.

36. **times.** The only place you can use a comma in this sentence is after the introductory phrase *At other times.*

37. **exceptable.** *Exceptable* may sound like a word, but it's not. The correct word to use is *acceptable.*

The more reading you do as you prepare for the test, the better your chances are for recognizing misspellings.

38. **A. Whatever the problem,.** A gift for you: No correction is required.

    If you chose Choice (D), keep in mind that this sentence has one subject and two verbs. These types of sentences don't require a comma between the two verbs. Not sure about subjects and verbs? Here, the subject is *step,* and the two verbs are *begins* and *gives.* If the sentence had a second subject before the second verb, it would need a comma.

39. **B. revise to read** *the cart before the horse.* If you live anywhere near Amish country, you know that the horse comes before the cart. Or you may have heard the idiomatic expression, "Don't put the cart before the horse." In either case, the proper correction is to reverse the order of *horse* and *cart.*

40. **Its.** *Its* is possessive (meaning that it shows that something belongs to *it*), whereas *it's* stands for "it is." Here, the sentence clearly means "it is."

    Confusing these two words is a common error that's usually tested in some way. Master the difference between *its* and *it's. It's* means "it is" and is often confused with the possessive form of other words that use the apostrophe.

41. **C. on the recovery front and further.** *Farther* always refers to distance. *Further* is a matter of degree. Here, you want degree, not distance.

    If you didn't know the answer, this question is a good example of one that you could answer by intelligent guessing. Choice (A) isn't correct because *with* isn't the proper word in this case. Choice (B) doesn't make sense in the context of the sentence. So now you just need to guess between Choices (C) and (D).

42. **not.** Commas used in moderation help sentences. Extra commas hurt sentences. In this sentence, the only comma used properly separates the introductory phrase *More often than not* from the rest of the sentence.

43. **C. change** *resource* **to** *Resource.* In the letter, the *York Square Employment Resource Center* is a title; as such, all words (except prepositions and articles) are capitalized.

44. **A. move** *since April 2002* **to the start of the sentence.** Moving *since April 2002* is the only good answer here. The current sentence sounds as though the training programs have been in existence since April 2002 when, in fact, the partnership has been in existence since that time.

45. **programs.** Most (although not all) lists begin with a colon. Because this is a bulleted list, and the list starts after the word *programs,* that is where the colon must be placed.

46. **A. has always been.** No correction is required.

47. **B. change** *are* **to** *is.* The subject of the sentence is *fact,* which is singular, but the verb is *are,* which is plural. Verbs must agree with their subjects.

48. **C. move** *, with a high degree of professional competence and efficiency* **to the end of the sentence after** *responsibilities.* In its current form, this sentence forces the reader to pause too long and remember too much. Rewriting it as "She has pursued her responsibilities with a high degree of professional competence and efficiency" is far more straightforward.

49. **A. add a comma after** *Peta.* As is, this sentence is a run-on sentence. To make it a compound sentence, all you have to do is add a comma after *Peta.*

50. **grimly ordinary.** The description states that it was like any other winter school day in Chicago — grimly ordinary.

51. **D. His mother was sick.** Louie was living with his mother, who was very ill and confined to bed. Other answers describing Louie's breakfast, his books, and his complexion aren't good descriptions of the focus of his home life.

52. **A. hunting for game.** The men were hunting pigeons (game) for food. You can see that having target practice, staying out of the weather, and hiding from the police are inappropriate answers. They aren't the key points, if you've read the passage thoroughly.

53. **D. It reinforces the image of great hardship, that people had to hunt pigeons for food in the cities.** The whole scene is grim, but only in that term do you realize the time setting is the Great Depression. That then reinforced the grimness of the scene. Although the men may be depressed and the weather bad, those things have nothing to do with the question. And although Choice (B) may be true, it doesn't answer the question, either.

54. **hungry.** The hunters and their families must have been hungry for food to hunt pigeons in the street.

55. **C. It had nothing to do with him.** What Louie saw had nothing to do with him, and he didn't want to get involved. Other possible answers — that he was hurrying to school, his mother was sick, or he was friends with the guys — don't relate to why Louie wouldn't tell the police.

56. **D. a camera.** The batteries are installed in a camera. Other answer choices, such as electronics or a children's toy, have no meaning in this excerpt. Point-and-shoot, while another term for a camera, isn't the best answer, because not all cameras are point-and-shoot.

57. **B. big point-and-shoots.** The easiest model in which to replace batteries is the point-and-shoot camera. The other answer choices — compact models, screw bottoms, and different types of covers — don't relate directly to the question.

58. **D. The battery cover may be lost.** Avoid all the locations mentioned so you don't lose your battery cover if you drop it. Sewer grates and tall grass are places where the cover could easily be lost. The rest of the answer choices refer to issues other than losing battery covers.

59. **D. Find a diagram.** To ensure that the batteries are correctly oriented, you must find the diagram and use it. Other choices, such as using four AAs or a single lithium or emptying the compartment, don't answer the question.

60. **B. the battery icon.** You must check the battery icon to see whether the batteries are low. LCD panels show a variety of information, so that option is not the best choice. According to the passage, battery compartment and lithium battery aren't correct answers.

Answers for Section 2, Social Studies

1. **D. They all exchanged products.** England, Africa, and the West Indies all traded products: The West Indies traded molasses, sugar, and slaves with England for food and wood; England (via the New England colonies) then made the molasses and sugar into rum and traded it with Africa for more slaves.

2. **C. purchase of slaves.** Rum was used to purchase slaves for use in the colonies. The other answer choices — colonial farms, milling of lumber, and molasses and sugar — were all patterns of commerce but weren't uses of rum.

3. **A. They built the ships.** Ships were built in the colonies to increase Atlantic trade. Sewing sails, naval stores, milled lumber, and other crafts were products of the colonies that ship-building stimulated, but ships were the primary reason the colonies were important to the Atlantic trade — the other choices were secondary.

4. **D. They provided raw materials.** The colonies provided raw materials for British manufacturing industries. According to the passage, "Mercantile theory encouraged the colonies to provide raw materials for England's industrializing economy. . . ."

5. **C. hats.** The export of hats — a finished good — from the colonies was prohibited because it threatened British manufacturing. Coal, pig iron, and lumber, were all raw materials, which didn't threaten English manufacturing.

6. **B. failing to pass laws.** According to the first paragraph of the passage, the king neglected the colonies in a number of ways. Of the ways listed here, only failing to pass laws (ones that would alleviate grievances) is correct. Although the other choices are grievances, they can't be alleviated until the appropriate laws are passed.

7. **D. He made them comply with his wishes.** According to the third paragraph of the passage, the legislative bodies were forced to comply with the king's rule (". . . for the sole purpose of fatiguing them into compliance with his measures . . .").

8. **A. He dissolved representative houses.** According to the fourth paragraph of the passage, when the king dissolved the representative houses, he threatened the rights of the people.

9. **D. discouraged people from settling.** The sixth paragraph of the passage says, "He has endeavored to prevent the population of these states." In other words, he has discouraged newcomers from settling.

10. **C. He refused to enact certain laws.** The seventh paragraph of the passage states that the king didn't give his approval to laws that would've created a local judicial system.

11. **an independent military.** The king made sure the military was independent from the colonists (last paragraph). This independence meant the colonists didn't have any authority over when to hire or fire soldiers, how large the military was, or who the officers were. Only the king made those kinds of decisions.

12. **D. Insufficient information is provided.** Although both Choices (A) and (B) are potentially correct, nothing in the map supports those statements. Choice (C) is simply speculation and, therefore, doesn't apply. The only option is Choice (D).

13. **C. 400,000.** You're asked for an approximate answer. First, find that the range of the male population is between 43.2% and 48.9%. So using an average of 47%, there are about 2.6 million males. That means that there are some 3 million females, for a surplus of about 400,000 females. Because all the numbers are approximate, you can round off your answer. Regardless, the only choice that comes close is Choice (C).

14. **White Male.** Based on the table, the group with the highest income for full-time employment for the year is White Male.

15. **B. Female, American Indian and Alaskan Native.** Based on the chart, the lowest full-time earners are American Indians and Alaskan native females.

16. **D. He could not.** The table doesn't list information for people under the age of 16. That is shown in the subheading of the chart title.

17. **C. liberty and equality.** As stated in the first two sentences of the passage, the issues of prime importance in the Civil War were liberty and equality. *Happiness and friendship, safety and security,* and *peace and prosperity* aren't the best answers.

18. **C. on a battlefield.** You know from the passage that President Lincoln was delivering his speech on a battlefield at Gettysburg. This fact rules out every answer choice except *on a battlefield* and *on the radio* (he could've recorded his speech, and it could've been broadcasted by radio at the battlefield). However, Lincoln gave this speech in 1863, and radios hadn't yet been invented.

19. **D. People around the world will not remember the speech.** Lincoln was saying that the world would remember the soldiers who died but would not remember his speech. (He was wrong, given that the Gettysburg Address is one of the most famous speeches in American history.)

20. **burial ground.** Some of the battlefield was to become a burial ground for the fallen.

21. **B. those who fought there.** The ground was hallowed by those who fought there. Lincoln doesn't believe the people involved in the dedication of the battlefield can make the place holy or important; only the people who fought on the battlefield can do so.

22. **C. time.** The word *years* follows *four score and seven,* so you can assume that phrase relates to time. (By the way, a score is 20 years, so four score and seven is 87 years.)

23. **Serbia.** Archduke Ferdinand was assassinated by a Serbian nationalist, so the correct answer is Serbia.

24. **B. demanding indemnities.** Austria demanded indemnities in response to the assassination. This answer comes directly from the passage.

25. **C. Germany and France.** Germany and France weren't allies in the war. Although the list of allies is rather confusing, the passage does sum up who was on which side.

26. **A. Germany invaded Belgium.** You know that Great Britain entered the war when Germany invaded Belgium from the sentence that states, "Great Britain entered the war on August 4, following Germany's invasion of neutral Belgium."

27. **C. Germany.** Germany was not an Allied power. About halfway through the passage is a list of the Central powers (on one side of the war) and the Allied powers (on the other side).

28. **B, D, C, A. Germany declares war on Russia; Germany invades Belgium; Great Britain declares war on Germany; Italy enters on the Allied side.** In this sequence, Germany declared war on Russia and then invaded Belgium. Great Britain declared war on Germany because it invaded Belgium. Italy didn't enter into the war on the Allied side until 1915.

29. **B. inspiring teacher.** In the cartoon, Barack Obama is portrayed in front of a chalkboard in a classroom setting. Most of the students are seen as receptive to his role as an inspiring teacher. The other choices — comedian, disciplinarian, or fashion model — don't go with the cartoon.

30. **D. issues that can be solved.** Most of the young people are portrayed as smiling students. They each represent an issue Obama must face, some more obvious than others. They're not happy voters, nor is there any indication that represents the public in general. Although they may represent a bright future, there are also problems, so Choice (D) is the most logical answer. The smiling faces reinforce the idea that these issues can be solved.

31. **A. These issues are very important but often overlooked.** Each of the students in the cartoon represents a different problem facing America, but the issue of tensions with Iran and

Iraq are always in the background and potentially a much larger problem for the president. The smiling faces suggest that the problems attached to them can be solved. But the issues of Iran and Iraq must also be solved, and the suggestion in the cartoon is that they're just waiting to become major.

32. **D. all of the above.** *All of the above* is the only correct choice because each of the students represents one of the problems facing America.

33. **34.6%.** According to the table, the United States produced 34.6% of the soybean output that year. It's the third item down on the last column of the table.

34. **B. most of it.** Production that year was 18.1 million bales. Exports amounted to 15.5 million bales. That is just over 85%. The best match among the choices is *most of it.*

35. **A. increased.** According to the table, center section, corn exports increased from 76.9 to 90.6 metric tons.

36. **480 pounds.** The explanatory notes under the table give the answer: 480 pounds.

37. **B. value of gold.** The first item on the list states "gold standard for currency adopted." That means that the value of the American dollar was based on the value of gold.

38. **A. It was the trigger.** The Great Depression was caused by a variety of issues, but the immediate cause, the trigger, was the crash of the stock market. The other answers are wrong. While Choice (B) says that problems had been building for a while, the crash started the panic that resulted in the Great Depression. It wasn't coincidence nor did the crash delay the Depression.

39. **D. Citizens had to take all their gold to government offices.** U.S. citizens had to take all their gold to U.S. offices and not keep any in their own homes. The timeline and graph don't tell you why they had to do so, just that they did. *Turn in* is the key phrase here.

40. **1973.** The U.S. currency was removed from the gold standard in 1973.

41. **C. The Soviet Union invaded Afghanistan.** The best answer is that gold reached a historic high when the Soviets invaded Afghanistan. You have to read the timeline to answer this question.

42. **A. Location. Meteorologists call these storms hurricanes in the Atlantic and northeast Pacific and cyclones in the eastern Pacific and Indian Ocean.** There is no difference between these storms other than location. Both hurricanes and cyclones are cyclonic storms, and both may bring flooding and heavy rains.

    A cyclone is not a tornado.

43. **D. Choices A and B.** The extreme drought conditions in Australia led to both crop failures and the need to sell off far more sheep than usual. Both represent financial losses. Therefore, Choices (A) and (B) are correct. Although Choice (C) may be true, no information offered supports the idea that crop insurance exists for these farmers.

44. **A. They reinforce the idea of climate change and global warming.** Because of unseasonably warm weather, locusts were found in Denmark. Locusts are drawn to warm weather. The fact that Denmark is warm enough to allow locusts to survive means that the local climate must be warming. Although the newscast doesn't say so, in the context of all the other information presented, this fact supports the argument of climate change. You must interpret the information to arrive at the correct conclusion.

45. **C. It was limited because of pre-war budget cuts.** The efforts against sabotage, Choice (A), and psychological warfare, Choice (D), weren't part of foreign intelligence gathering and are thus wrong. Choice (B) is also domestic intelligence. The foreign intelligence work was limited because of budget issues. The text states at the end of the first paragraph that foreign intelligence "did not aid the cause very much."

Answers for Section 3, Science

1. **B. Replace the floor-to-ceiling window with a cinder block wall.** Glass contains no encapsulated air and, thus, provides neither insulation nor greater thermal flow. To answer this question, you need to know that good insulators contain trapped air and that glass doesn't. Thus, replacing the floor-to-ceiling glass walls with a cinder block wall would increase the insulating properties of that wall and reduce the heating costs for the house. The question assumes that this information is general knowledge for someone at this educational level.

2. **C. Wear clothing with thermal padding in the house.** Each of the options would reduce heat loss and reduce energy costs. General knowledge would let you assume that Juno was considerably warmer during the summer, and the word *thermal* indicates a garment that's meant to reduce personal heat loss and, thus, would allow the room temperature to be reduced.

3. **D. Plants provide animals with chemical potential energy.** The last paragraph of the passage implies that animals must eat food with chemical potential energy, which is derived from plants. The other answers are irrelevant to the information in the passage.

4. **D. The plant would starve to death.** Plants produce food using energy from the sun. If you cut off the energy from the sun, you cut off the food supply. The other answers may be symptoms of a plant's starving to death, but Choice (D) sums up the information in one answer.

5. **pyruvic acid.** According to the passage, pyruvic acid is key to energy production. This question is a good example of why a little bit of knowledge and familiarity with the words and names used in science are helpful when taking the GED test.

6. **D. vector.** The passage states that velocity can be represented by a vector because it has both magnitude and direction. Force is defined as changing the state or motion of an object, either in magnitude or direction. Because a force has magnitude and direction, it's represented by a vector. The information needed to answer this question is in the last sentence of the first paragraph. You can ignore the first three answer choices completely because they have very little to do with the question. Choice (D) requires you to know the difference between a vector and a scalar. The last line of each paragraph in the passage contains the definitions you need.

7. **vectors.** Because the GPS gives directions containing both magnitude and direction, the directions would really be in the form of vectors.

8. **B. Steam condenses when cooled, occupying less space.** In the steam engine, water cools the steam, which then condenses, occupying less space. This action starts the entire cycle over again. You can eliminate the other answer choices when guessing is necessary. Choice (A) is incorrect because water and steam are both water, in different states. Their densities may be different, but their weights are the same. Only the volume differs when water turns to steam. Choice (C) is incorrect because the boiler doesn't provide the energy to move the pump, which you can see by looking at the diagram. Choice (D) isn't based on information given in the diagram. Nowhere are you told the weight of the pump rod.

9. **C. It causes the pump to fill the cistern with water.** The pump pushes water into the cistern. The other choices don't answer the question based on the information provided in the diagram. Knowing how to answer questions based on diagrams is a useful skill to have for the GED test.

10. **consumers would starve for lack of food.** The producers provide food for the consumers. If the producers stay the same but the consumers increase, the consumers won't have enough food, so the consumers will starve. Your reading in science topics should have exposed you to this concept. If you read the newspapers regularly, you'll find stories about the lack of food leading to starvation, which is a semi-scientific statement of this principle.

11. **10.** The passage states that the temperature of the first tiny particles was 10 billion degrees.

12. **D. gravity.** The last paragraph states that gravity transformed the atoms into galaxies. This question is an example of when a basic knowledge of science-related words can be helpful.

13. **B. An immense explosion created the planets.** The passage states that immense explosions created the planets when the space debris was attracted to each other by gravity.

14. **D. Both are nuclear reactions.** An atomic bomb uses a nuclear reaction to produce its massive damage. The passage states that hydrogen and helium atoms were formed by nuclear reactions (Choice [D]). The other three choices don't answer the question based on the passage. Choice (A) may be right, but it's irrelevant in this context. Choice (B) is incorrect, and Choice (C) may be interesting in another context, but it's wrong here.

15. **D. It has no backbone.** According to the passage (second sentence in the first paragraph), invertebrates have no backbones. The other choices may be correct, but they don't answer the question. Here, and in all questions on this test, you're looking for the best answer that answers the question posed. Don't get sidetracked by other choices that are correct based on your knowledge or even based on the passage. The answer to the question posed is always the best response on a multiple-choice test.

16. **D. The jellyfish may sting the swimmer, and the stings are painful.** Jellyfish can sting swimmers, and the stings are painful. You find this information in the last sentence of the third paragraph. The other choices don't answer the question based on the passage. For example, Choice (C) may be the stuff nightmares are based on, but the information or misinformation isn't in the passage, so you can't consider it.

17. **B. Jellyfish sting and eat small ocean creatures.** Small ocean creatures are always on the menu for jellyfish. Creatures, in general, avoid predators — a fact that's general science knowledge.

18. **B. The energy in the lightning must be conserved and is transformed into another form of energy that affects the tree.** The passage states that energy can't be created or destroyed, so the energy from the lightning must be transformed into another type of energy. The other answer choices imply that the energy has somehow disappeared, which the passage says can't happen.

19. **D. All of the above.** Science is an ordered discipline and, as such, needs laws to maintain its organization.

20. **C. creation of illusion.** Matter can't be created or destroyed. Thus, a rabbit can't appear except by creation of an illusion, which isn't a true law of science but the best answer of the choices given. The other answer choices seem scientific but have nothing to do with the question. Always read the question carefully to make sure you're answering it with the best of the answers provided.

21. **conservation of matter.** When ice melts, it turns into water. This is an example of the law of conservation of matter. Although the amount of water in a melting iceberg is tiny compared to the amount of water in the ocean, it does add some water to the ocean, which may be considered another acceptable answer but not the best one.

22. **A. It has been converted into light.** Flashlights provide light by using the energy in the battery. The passage says that energy can't be created or destroyed, so the energy in the battery must have been converted or transformed into something else. In reality, even if you don't use a battery for an extended time, the battery grows weaker because of other reactions inside the cell. But this tidbit isn't mentioned in the passage and is just a reminder not to leave batteries in your flashlight forever.

23. **D. An example of the law of conservation of mass in that the total mass will remain the same.** If you add 3 ounces of water to 1 ounce of salt, you have 4 ounces of combined ingredients. The combined mass is the same as the sum of the individual masses. The volume may be different, but the question doesn't ask you about the volume. If you add 3 ounces of water

to a dissolvable substance, you'll get at least 3 ounces of resultant liquid, but that isn't what was asked in the question. Choices (A) and (C) are just incorrect.

24. **C. The energy from rolling down the hill can't disappear.** The law of conservation of energy states that energy can't be created or destroyed. Thus, the energy developed by the ball rolling down the hill can't disappear. Choice (C) is more a statement of the meaning of the law of conservation of energy than naming it, but it is still the best answer. In reality, there's friction between the ball and the ground that slows it down, and the hills don't go on forever — so the ball will eventually come to rest. You may have learned this information elsewhere, but it doesn't answer the question based on the passage.

25. **D. All of the above.** Choices (A), (B), and (C) contribute to a definition of a scientific law, so Choice (D) is the best answer because it indicated that the others are a summary.

26. **C. They are able to find food again.** The passage states that the lack of food in the winter months makes most birds fly south to find sources of food. When the food returns to the northern states, so do the birds. The other choices don't answer the question based on the information in the passage.

27. **C. Some birds eat insects.** Some birds eat insects for their food supply. If an area has no insects, the birds move to find a new source of food. General reading in science tells you that living creatures go where the food is. Even human beings, who can choose where to live, are unlikely to move somewhere that lacks food. Other creatures have a more basic instinct to move to where there's a supply of food. Thus, the insects have a responsibility for the birds' migration — although their main contribution is being eaten.

28. **A. It happens regularly and apparently without reason.** Scientists are curious about anything that happens regularly that can't be easily explained. Migration is one such issue. The key word here is *every* at the beginning of the first sentence.

29. **D. the Nile Perch.** This question may have many answers, from sport fishermen to algae to snails. Of the potential answers given, however, Nile Perch is the best one because the introduction of this species caused all the subsequent problems.

30. **D. The foreign species can upset the ecological balance.** This question asks you to make a general statement about foreign species of fish. Although this question doesn't ask you specifically to consider the Lake Victoria example, you're supposed to think about that example as you answer the question. Using the Lake Victoria example, you can safely say that a foreign species upsets the local ecological balance. You also know from the example that the other three choices are incorrect.

31. **A. Lower gravity on the moon means you need less fuel for the launch.** The less fuel you need to launch, the less you have to carry. The gravity on the moon is less than that on Earth, so you need less force and less fuel to break free of gravity.

32. **D. not enough information given.** The only locations mentioned in the table are Mars and the moon, and you're supposed to answer the question based on the material given. Thus, you don't have enough information to answer the question.

33. **B. The time of the trip is much shorter.** According to the table, it takes just 3 days to get to the moon, which is a much better first choice than the 1.88 years needed to get to Mars. The other choices are irrelevant to the question and the given table.

34. **the moon.** Gravity on the moon is less than that on Mars. Because gravity is the force that attracts you to the moon (or to Earth or to Mars), the less the gravity, the less the attraction between you and the surface on which you stand, and, thus, the higher and farther you can jump — which, as you may know, is the goal of a pole-vaulting contest.

35. **heredity.** The passage states that heredity determines the characteristics of the next generation.

36. **C. genetic code.** The passage states, "These characteristics, passed from one generation to the next, exist because of genetic code." Thus, the best answer is *genetic code*.

37. **B. monster-sized pumpkins.** If children inherit the traits of their parents, you want the desired traits of your child pumpkin to be a part of the traits of the parent pumpkins.

Monster-sized pumpkin seeds have a better chance of producing extra large pumpkins than do the seeds from a regular-sized pumpkin.

38. **D. because it is no longer needed.** All the choices except Choice (D) — that the booster is no longer needed — are incorrect because they're in direct opposition to the passage. If you can quickly eliminate some or most of the answer choices, you can save time answering the question. In this case, you can eliminate three answers, making the final choice easy and quick.

39. **C. orbiter.** Because the booster is jettisoned after takeoff, the orbiter has to carry everything that continues on the trip. Choices (A), (B), and (D) are wrong and can be quickly eliminated.

40. **B. The hand would move downward.** If the force pushing down is greater than the force pushing up, the hand would move down. Although this question is based on the given diagram, which gives a general idea of what happens when a hand holds weight, the answer to the question is in the first part of the question itself. If the force of gravity (the downward force) is greater than the force of the muscles moving upward, the resultant force would be downward.

41. **B. adding weight to the hand.** A larger weight in the hand would produce a greater force downward. Thus, the athlete would have to work harder against this extra weight (and, as a result, would build more muscle). Making the displacement of the hand larger would also increase the work done, but this isn't an answer choice.

42. **heat.** The fourth sentence in the passage tells you that heating is the process that separates DNA strands. The other choices either don't answer the question or are wrong.

43. **it creates an identical copy of the DNA.** Cloning requires identical DNA. As you can see from the first sentence of the passage, PCR provides identical copies of DNA.

44. **C. larger teeth.** The larger teeth of the wolf are better for hunting. The third sentence of the third paragraph of the passage states that dogs have smaller teeth, which means wolves must have bigger teeth. Although this information isn't stated directly in the passage, it's implied. You're expected to be able to draw conclusions from the information given, so read carefully. The other answer choices are incorrect. True, some dogs have heavier coats, larger bodies, and so on, but this information isn't in the passage. You can answer the question using only information given or implied in the passage — not information from your general knowledge or prior reading.

45. **B. Dogs were domesticated.** The passage states that the dog was domesticated very long ago. A domesticated animal is preferable to a wild one for a household pet. The other answers may be factually correct, but they aren't part of the information included in the passage.

46. **protons.** According to the first sentence of the passage, the atomic number is determined by the number of protons. Skimming the paragraph after reading the question for key words in the question makes choosing the correct answer faster and easier.

47. **C. atomic number.** The last sentence of the first paragraph of the passage states that isotopes have the same atomic number.

48. **B. They are isotopes.** The last sentence of the first paragraph of the passage states that isotopes have the same atomic number. The second sentence of the second paragraph tells you that isotopes have different mass numbers. This question requires using two bits of information from two different locations in the passage to decide on the right answer.

49. **D. Find a safe shelter and hibernate.** According to the first sentence of the second paragraph of the passage, animals, including bears, survive the winter by finding a safe shelter and hibernating.

50. **D. It would not be able to find enough food to survive.** Animals hibernate in the winter when food is scarce (a fact implied from the last sentence in the second paragraph). If you wake up a hibernating animal, that animal awakes to a strange environment without its usual sources of food and probably wouldn't be able to find enough food to survive. The other answer choices may be right in some circumstances, but they don't relate to the passage.

Answers for Section 4, Mathematical Reasoning

1. **C. Sign D offers the worst deal.** This problem tests your understanding of numbers and their equivalents (integers, fractions, decimals, and percents) in a real-world situation. Signs A, B, and C give customers 50% off. Sign D gives them 45% (9 × 5% sales tax). Sign D offers the least discount.

2. **A. *ab* must be perpendicular to *ad*.** This problem involves measurement and geometry and tests your understanding of perpendicular and parallel lines in a geometrical figure. Frames are rectangles. Each pair of opposite sides must be parallel and intersecting sides (*ab* and *ad*) must be perpendicular..

3. **$1,680.** This problem tests your knowledge and mastery of number operations and number sense. Use a calculator, because numerous conversions are involved, including the following:

    Area of the deck is 16 × 21 = 336 square feet

    9 square feet = 1 square yard

    $\frac{336}{9} = 37\frac{1}{3}$ square yards

    1 square yard of decking costs $45.00.

    $37\frac{1}{3}$ square yards of decking costs $1,680.00.

4. **B. grommets.** This problem tests your data-analysis skills. You're asked to interpret and draw inferences from the bar graph and include additional data from the presentation. Because the profit per unit is the same for grommets and gadgets but differs from the profit on widgets, which had twice the profitability, to make a fair comparison, you'd have to double the sales of widgets. In this case, grommets seem to be less profitable than the other two lines but not by much. Because grommets sold the fewest numbers and were the least profitable product, they're recommended as the one to drop.

5. **average.** This problem tests your skills in calculations of statistical measurement. You're asked to use the presented data to calculate the measures of Quan's performance and compare them to those of his classmates. This is a good question on which to use the calculator because it involves a series of calculations.

    You find the *average* by adding the marks and dividing by the total number of marks. The *median* is the middle value; in Quan's case, the middle value is the fourth value, which just happens to be equal to the fifth value. The *mode* is the most often, or common, value in the list, and the *range* is the difference between the largest and smallest numbers. This question is a good example of why some familiarity with mathematical vocabulary is an asset. The admissions department of a college would put the most weight on Quan's average because it's a reflection of how well he did in all his subjects.

6. **A. June.** Alice has converted her story into a graph, and you're being asked to interpret the line graph in conjunction with her story. Because her average daily time had been increasing until May, dropped in June, and recovered in July and August, you can assume that the twisted ankle slowed her down. It likely happened in June.

7. **D. 19:18.** Number operations are involved in solving this problem. You're asked to average a set of grades for each person and compare them by using a ratio. You can simplify this question, using a calculator.

    The total of Paula's marks is 80 + 64 + 76 + 72 + 88 = 380.

    The total of Dominic's marks is 63 + 76 + 65 + 84 + 72 = 360.

    Because you divide each total by 5 to get the averages for Paula and Dominic, you can simply use the ratio of the totals to get the answer because it will equal the ratio of the averages. (Note that if one of the students had six grades and the other had five, for example, you'd have to use the ratio of the averages, not of the totals.)

    The ratio of Paula's marks to Dominic's marks is 380:360, which you can simplify by dividing each number by 20 to get 19:18.

8. **66.** This problem involves algebra, functions, and patterns. The numbers 4, 6, 10, and 18 form a pattern (also called a series). After looking carefully at the series, you see that the second term is formed by subtracting 1 from the first term and multiplying by 2. Try this on the third number: $(6 - 1) \times 2 = 10$. You've found your pattern. Continuing the series: 4, 6, 10, 18, 34, 66, . . . , the first term you come to that is a multiple of 11 is 66.

9. **B. $16.13.** This problem involves data analysis and manipulation of numbers and is best done using a calculator. Most of the information given is irrelevant, except to decide that Simone may have bought at a high point. The important price to consider is $15.19. In addition to this price per share, Simone has to pay her broker 3% commission.

Therefore, her final price per share on September 24 is $15.19 + (0.03 \times $15.19) = $15.6457. Because you're dealing with money, you have to round the number to two decimal places, making her final price per share $15.65. This amount of money came out of her bank account for each share she bought.

If Simone decides to sell the shares at this price, $15.65, she has to pay her broker another 3% commission, or $0.03 \times $15.65 = $0.4695. Rounded to two decimals, she has to pay a commission of $0.47 per share. She then receives the value of the shares, $15.65, minus the commission of $0.47, for a total of $15.18 per share — that is, for each share she sells, the broker deposits $15.18 into her account. Notice that this amount is less than the amount she paid for each share.

To break even, Simone has to receive $15.65 per share — after the commission. Set the equation up this way:

$1x - x(0.03) = 15.65$, where x is the selling price

$1x - 0.03x = 15.65$

$0.97x = 15.65$

Now divide both sides by 0.97 to get $x = 16.13$.

10. **D. –4.** This question involves algebra. You have to solve a linear equation, as follows:

$$22.4 = \frac{56a}{5a+10}$$

Cross-multiply and write this equation as $22.4(5a + 10) = 56a$.

Getting rid of the parentheses, the equation looks like this: $112a + 224 = 56a$.

Bringing all the a's to the left and the numbers to the right, you have $112a - 56a = -224$.

Combining the a's, you have $56a = -224$.

Divide both sides by 56 to get one a on the left: $a = -4$.

11. **2/3.** This question tests your skills in measurement and geometry. You're asked to find the slope of a line drawn for you.

The x-axis runs horizontally across the grid. The y-axis runs vertically, up and down the grid. The origin is where the two axes (that's the plural of axis) intersect. Points to the left of the y-axis have negative x-values. Points below the x-axis have negative y-values. The x-intercept of a line is the point where the line cuts the x-axis. The y-intercept of a line is the point where the line cuts the y-axis. All lines parallel to the x-axis have slopes of 0.

The slope of a line is the rise over the run. The rise is 4, and the run is 6. This means that the slope is 4/6 or 2/3 (divide by 2 to simplify).

12. **(–6, 0).** This question tests your skills in measurement and geometry. You're asked to identify the x-intercept and the y-intercept and to draw a line with a slope of 2/3 on the graph.

If you draw a line through the point on the y-axis having the same slope, it crosses the x-axis at (–6, 0). Simply count over 3 points to the left (the run), down 2 (the rise), and you're at (–3, 2). But you're asked for the x-intercept, so repeat this process. Go over 3 more points to the left and down 2 more, and you're at (–6, 0).

13. **D. not enough information given.** This question doesn't provide enough information for you to give an accurate answer. If the fire were rectangular in shape, the answer would be different from a circular fire or an irregularly shaped fire. The question provides information only about the shape of the barbeque.

14. **C. $2.19.** Consider the price per square foot at each store:

    Carnie's Carpets: $21.50 per square yard = $21.50/9 = $2.39 per square foot

    Flora's Flooring: $2.45 per square foot

    Dora's Deep Discount: The area of an 8-x-12-foot rug is (8)(12) = 96 square feet. The cost for 96 square feet is $210.24 or $210.24/96 = $2.19 per square foot.

15. **A. third quarter.** In this question, you're asked to analyze graphs to identify patterns in a workplace situation.

    In the 2013 graph, the third quarter of 2013 produces a little more than 30% of the output. The best answer for this question is the third quarter.

16. **1,140.** This problem involves measurement, specifically, area and money. Assuming that the estimate for renovation is accurate, the number of square feet of renovation that the Ngs can afford for $18,000 is $18,000/15.80 square feet = 1,139.24 square feet. Round this number to 1,140 because you usually don't add part of a square foot.

17. **(6, 6).** This problem involves data analysis, statistics, and probability. You're being asked to graph a point representing the medians of two sets of data. First, find the median (the middle number, when put in order) of the first set of numbers. The median is 6. Then find the median of the second set of numbers. Again, it's 6.

18. **B. sedan.** This problem is based on measurement using uniform rates, and it asks you to make a decision based on factual information. To figure the cost of gasoline over the five years, set up the problem this way:

    $$18{,}000 \text{ miles} \times \frac{1 \text{ gallon}}{12.8 \text{ miles}} \times \frac{\$3.50}{\text{gallon}} \times 5 \text{ years}$$

    To help you decide which car LeeAnne should buy, create a chart like the following:

Vehicle Type	Miles/Gallon	Total Gas Costs
SUV	12.8	$24,609.38
Sedan	19.6	$16,071.43
2-door	19.5	$16,153.83
All-wheel drive	17.2	$18,313.94
Sports car	18.6	$16,935.47

    From these figures, you can see that the sedan is the best buy.

19. **C. divide then add.** This problem involves number operations. Instead of asking you for the answer, which is pretty simple, you're asked to provide the operations that are required to solve the problem. First, you divide (miles to site by miles per hour), and then you add (the amount of time Tom wants to arrive early). Remember to keep the units consistent.

20. **D. 11.** This question involves data analysis. You're asked to apply measures of central tendency (the mean) and analyze the effect of changes in data on this measure. If Leonora's present average is 77.8% and she wants to get an average of 80%, she needs enough marks to get an additional 2.2% (80 – 77.8).

Because Leonora is taking five subjects, she requires 5 extra points for each percent increase. Thus, she requires (2.2)(5) = 11 additional points. The problem says that English is her best subject, so she would need the 11 extra points in English.

21. **A. 7 cups of soup and ⅞ cup of lentils.** This question tests your ability to figure out how a change in the amount of rice used results in changes to the amount of soup and lentils needed.

Because each cup of rice requires 2 cups of soup, 3½ cups of rice require 2 × 3½ = 7 cups of soup.

Because each cup of rice requires ¼ cup of lentils, 3½ cups of rice require 3½ × ¼ = 7⁄2 × ¼ = ⅞ cup of lentils.

22. **C. 1:46.** This question is a test in probability. You're asked to figure out the probability of an event occurring. If you had an entire deck of 52 cards, the probability of drawing an ace of hearts would be 1:52. If you remove 6 cards and none of them is the ace of hearts, you may as well have a 46-card deck (52 – 6). The probability of drawing an ace of hearts from a 46-card deck is 1:46.

23. **B. the larger rug.** This problem tests your measurement skills. You're asked to predict the impact of changes in the linear dimensions of the rug on its area and cost. Choice (C) seems logical, but the question never mentions the cost of the paneling or the skylight, so you can't consider it as an answer.

Draw a sketch of the room with the larger rug. It will have a tiled area around it. You have to figure out how many square feet of tile and carpet you need for this floor treatment, as follows:

The area of the room is (18)(12) = 216 square feet.

The larger rug will cover (16)(10) = 160 square feet of the floor. This leaves 56 square feet (216 – 160) to be covered with tile. The cost of the rug is ($7.50)(160) = $1,200. The cost of the tile is ($9.00)(56) = $504.00. The total cost is $1,200.00 + $504.00 = $1,704.00.

The smaller rug will cover (12)(8) = 96 square feet of the floor. This leaves 216 – 96 = 120 square feet to be covered with tile. The cost of the rug is ($7.50)(96) = $720.00. The cost of the tile is ($9.00)(120) = $1,080.00. The total cost is $720.00 + $1,080.00 = $1,800.00. The smaller rug will cost more for the entire floor treatment.

Tile costs more per square foot than carpeting, so you know without doing any figuring that having more tile will result in higher costs.

24. **C. loveseat.** This question is an exercise in data analysis. You're asked to compare sets of data based on the mean (average) prices of four other stores. You can summarize the average prices on a sketch table like this one:

Item	Store A	Store B	Store C	Store D	Average Price	Friendly Furniture
Couch	$1,729.00	$1,749.00	$1,729.00	$1,699.00	$1,726.50	$1,719.00
Dining room set	$4,999.00	$4,899.00	$5,019.00	$4,829.00	$4,936.50	$4,899.00
Loveseat	$1,259.00	$1,199.00	$1,279.00	$1,149.00	$1,221.50	$1,229.00
Coffee table	$459.00	$449.00	$479.00	$429.00	$454.00	$449.00
Reclining chair	$759.00	$799.00	$739.00	$699.00	$749.00	$739.00

You can see that the only item Friendly Furniture sells for over the average price is the loveseat, which is the answer to the question.

25. **320.** This question tests your knowledge of number operations by asking you to solve a problem involving calculations. Sarah ate 48/18 pistachios per minute. In 2 hours or 120 minutes, she could eat $120 \times \frac{48}{18} = 320$.

26. **multiplication.** This question is about number operations; it asks you to select the appropriate operation to solve a problem. Because the first operation performed is to find the volume of the room, and the formula for volume is *length × width × height,* the first operation you use to solve the problem is multiplication.

27. **D. not enough information given.** This question tests your knowledge of measurement and geometry. You're asked to visualize and describe geometrical figures under a 90-degree rotation. Each of the figures is changed by the rotation. Try drawing each of these shapes, picking a point on the perimeter and rotating it 90 degrees. Because this is a timed test, try drawing one or two, noticing that they change quite a bit. Use your imagination to check the rest. After discovering that none of the four shapes has the same relationship to the horizontal after a 90-degree rotation about a point on its perimeter, you have your answer — not enough information given.

28. **7:1.** This question tests your data-analysis skills by asking you to interpret a chart and answer a question involving calculation.

    The largest budget is the Operations budget, while the smallest budget is Human Resources. The ratio between these two budgets is 14.7 to 2.1 or 7:1 (dividing both sides by 2.1).

    If you wanted to do this in your head, notice that 14:2 (the approximate ratio between the Operations budget and the Human Resources budget) is double 7:1.

29. **5.** This question tests your knowledge of patterns by asking you to compare information from different types of graphs to extract information. Graph 5 has the first and third quarters in the required ratio.

30. **D. not enough information.** This problem involves measurement and geometry, and it asks you to use the Pythagorean theorem.

    You can't actually solve this problem, however. Because the rangefinder is measuring the distance from the forester's eye and you don't know how high his eye is above the ground, you can't calculate the height of the tree. You can calculate the distance from the forester's eye to the top of the tree by using the Pythagorean theorem, but the question asks for the height of the tree (which is the distance from the ground — not the forester's eye — to the top of the tree). Thus, you don't have enough information.

31. **$78.50.** This question tests your knowledge of number operations by asking you to perform several operations to calculate an answer. After the fourth week, Lawrie would've deposited (4)($24.00) = $96.00. There would've been two withdrawals totaling $7.50 + $10.00 = $17.50. Her balance after the fourth week would be $96.00 – $17.50 = $78.50.

32. **$3.20.** This question tests your skills in using percentages and discounts. Store A offers Sarah 1/3 off or 96/3 = $32.00 off the original price. Store B offers her 30% off; 30% is 0.30, so she'll get (96)(0.30) = $28.80 off the original price. By buying at Store A, she'd get the chair for $32.00 – $28.80 = $3.20 less. Thus, she'd save $3.20.

33. **D. 100.** This question tests your skills by asking you to use information from a graph to solve a problem. From the graph, you can figure out that the volume in decibels is the square of the volume setting. For a volume setting of 4, the volume is 16 decibels. Therefore, for a setting of 10, the volume is 100 decibels (10^2).

34. **D. 12.** This question tests your skills in algebra by asking you to solve equations. The equation given is $V = S^2$. If $S^2 = 144$, the square root of 144 is 12. Thus, the answer is 12.

35. **A. 36.** If the volume decreases by half for every 10 feet away from the stage you get and the volume at the stage is 144 decibels, a person sitting 10 feet from the stage would hear at a volume of 72 decibels (144/2), and a person sitting 20 feet from the stage would hear at a volume of 36 decibels (72/2).

36. **12.** This question involves number operations. You're asked to calculate the average miles per gallon for a vehicle. Rather than provide you with the number of gallons used, you're given the cost of gasoline and the cost of the 240-mile trip. To calculate the amount of fuel used, you divide $54.00 by $2.70 to get 20 gallons. You can do this operation mentally to speed things up. Next, you divide the miles, 240, by the fuel used, 20 gallons, to get the mileage, 12 miles per gallon (240/20 = 12).

37. **D. circle.** This question tests your skills in measurement and geometry. To remain at a constant temperature, you have to remain at a constant distance from the fire.

    The path of a point that travels a constant distance from a point is a circle.

38. **4.48.** This problem tests your ability to do calculations and use a formula: *Volume = length × width × depth*. Thus, 12,902 cubic feet = 120 feet × 24 feet × average depth. The average depth $= \dfrac{12,902}{(120 \times 24)} = 4.48$ (the answer is rounded).

39. **D. 2,949.** This question tests your ability to make a decision based on data presented in a table and then to use that information to answer a question. The least economical car costs $1,823 to drive for a year, while the most economical car costs $840 for the same time under the same conditions. The difference in cost for one year is $1,823 – $840 = $983. The cost for three years is ($983)(3) = $2,949.

40. **A. 1 2/3.** This question tests your ability to analyze data, using the mean and median to answer a question about the data given. The mean of the city mileages is the sum of the mileages divided by 10 (the number of entries), which equals 16.8. The median of the mileages is the one midway between the two in the middle, or 16.5. The difference between the two numbers (16.8 – 16.5) is 0.3 or 1/3.

41. **(0, 5).** This question tests your ability to analyze data by representing data graphically.

    For Vehicle A, the difference between the city and highway mileage is 5 miles per gallon (28 – 23). The point you want on the *y*-axis is (0, 5), which you need to mark on the graph.

42. **D. +8.** This question tests your skill in algebra by asking you to solve a system of linear equations:

    $2x + 3y = 10$

    $5x + 6y = 13$

    A linear equation is one in which the powers of the variables are all equal to 1. To solve this system, you have to eliminate *x* by multiplying each equation by a number that allows you to subtract one from the other and end up with just *y*'s. Multiply the first equation by 5 and the second equation by 2:

    $5(2x + 3y = 10) = 10x + 15y = 50$

    $2(5x + 6y = 13) = 10x + 12y = 26$

    Subtract the second equation from the first, and you get $3y = 24$; $y = 8$. (Note that you can also multiply the second equation by –2 and add the two equations together. Either way gets you the same answer.)

43. **B. 4 times as many.** This question asks you to analyze a situation presented in a table. The table tells you that the country with the highest participation rate is the United States, with a participation rate of 66.4. The country with the lowest participation rate is Portugal, with a participation rate of 15.5. Because you're asked for an approximation, you can say that the participation rate in the United States is 60 and in Portugal, it's 15, which means that 4 times as many adults participate in adult education in the United States than in Portugal.

44. **D. $18.00.** This problem involves number operations. The total amount of Gordon's bills is $23.00 + $31.00 + $48.00 + $13.00 + $114.00 + $39.00 = $268.00. If Gordon allocates only $250.00 to pay these bills, he ends up $268.00 – $250.00 = $18.00 short. Be wary of Choice (B), which is a special trap for people who don't read the question carefully.

45. **3 hours.** At the end of the first month, Georgette will owe $185 + $20 = $205. The second month's interest will be ($205)(0.15) = $30.75. At $11 an hour, Georgette would have to work an additional 2.76 hours, or practically 3 hours because no one would hire someone to work 2 hours, 45 minutes, and 36 seconds.

46. **D. approximately 5,300.** This problem tests your knowledge of measurement and geometry by asking you to solve a problem involving volume and weight. You can do this problem in your head, but we take you through the steps using calculations first.

    The formula for volume of a cylinder (the cylinder is the circular inside of the pool to a height of 9 inches) is $\pi r^2 h$, where π = approximately 3.14, r = radius, and h = height. If the diameter is 12 feet, the radius is 6 feet. If the height is 9 inches, it's 9/12 feet, which can be simplified to 3/4 feet.

    In a formula, don't forget that all units must be the same — that is, feet and feet or inches and inches.

    The volume is (3.14)[(6)(6)](3/4) = 85.59 cubic feet.

    Because 1 cubic foot weighs 62.42 pounds, the weight of 85.59 cubic feet is (85.59)(62.42) = 5,343 or 5,300 rounded to the nearest hundred.

    To do this problem in your head, multiply 6 by 6 to get 36. Multiply 36 by 3/4 to get 27, and multiply 27 by 3 to get 81. The approximate volume of the pool is 81 cubic feet, which isn't bad for an approximation. For your purposes, say the volume is 80 cubic feet, which is still close. The weight of a cubic foot of water is 62.42 pounds, so round it to 60 pounds. Now, multiply 80 by 60 to get 4,800, which is closest to Choice (D). You can go with that approximation because it's very close to one of the answers.

47. **A. 6.4%.** This question tests your ability to evaluate an answer by using a formula. This formula, $I = prt$, isn't in the format you want because you want to calculate the rate, which means solving for r. You can change the equation to $r = \dfrac{I}{p \times t}$, which allows you to calculate the rate from the information given. Substituting into this equation, you get $r = \dfrac{8}{100 \times 1.25}$. (Remember that 1 year and 3 months is 1 1/4, or 1.25 of a year.)

    Then $r = \dfrac{8}{125} = 0.064 = 6.4\%$.

48. **C. $4.90.** This question involves number operations. You're asked to calculate — in your head — the answer to a problem.

    To use mental math to solve this problem, round everything. Consider the apples at $0.80 a pound, bananas at $0.20 each, milk at $1.30, and a loaf of bread at $1.00. The total for this approximation is (2)($0.80) + (5)($0.20) + $1.30 + $1.00 = $4.90. Looking at the answer choices, Choice (C) is the only one close to this approximation.

49. **A. 28.** This question tests your knowledge of patterns by asking you to figure out the next number in a series. By looking at the series, it looks like each number is the square of the placement of the number in the list, plus 3. That is, the first number is 1^2 plus 3, or 4. The second number is 2^2 plus 3, or 7. The third term is 3^2 (9) plus 3, or 12. The fifth term would be 5^2 (25) plus 3, which is 28.

50. **C. (–2, –2).** This question tests your skills in geometry by asking you to visualize a graph of an object. Because the object is a rectangle, the opposite sides are equal in length and are parallel, the fourth corner will be 2 units to the left of the *y*-axis, giving it an *x*-coordinate of –2, and 2 units below the *x*-axis, giving it a *y*-coordinate of –2. Therefore, the point would be (–2, –2).

    The *x*-coordinate is the distance from the *y*-axis, and the *y*-coordinate is the distance from the *x*-axis.

Answer Key

Section 1: Reasoning Through Language Arts

1. B

2. C

3. distributing discarded materials to visual arts classes

4. B

5. D

6. C

7. A

8. D

9. B

10. D

11. A

12. C

13. B

14. B

15. D

16. A

17. B

18. C

19. B

20. D

21. B

22. D

23. C

24. Dutch colonists

25. A

26. yellow bricks

27. Hawkins's fields

28. A

29. D

30. B

31. A

32. B

33. D

34. A

35. C

36. times

37. exceptable

38. A

39. B

40. Its

41. C

42. not

43. C

44. A

45. programs

46. A

47. B

48. C

49. A

50. grimly ordinary

51. D

52. A

53. D

54. hungry

55. C

56. D

57. B

58. D

59. D

60. B

Section 2: Social Studies

1. D	16. D	31. A
2. C	17. C	32. D
3. A	18. C	33. **34.6%**
4. D	19. D	34. B
5. C	20. **burial ground**	35. A
6. B	21. B	36. **480 pounds**
7. D	22. C	37. B
8. A	23. **Serbia**	38. A
9. D	24. B	39. D
10. C	25. C	40. **1973**
11. **an independent military**	26. A	41. C
12. D	27. C	42. A
13. C	28. **B, D, C, A**	43. D
14. **White Male**	29. B	44. A
15. B	30. D	45. C

Section 3: Science

1. B
2. C
3. D
4. D
5. **pyruvic acid**
6. D
7. **vectors**
8. B
9. C
10. **consumer would starve for lack of food**
11. **10**
12. D
13. B
14. D
15. D
16. D
17. B
18. B
19. D
20. C
21. **conservation of matter**
22. A
23. D
24. C
25. D
26. C
27. C
28. A
29. D
30. D
31. A
32. D
33. B
34. **the moon**
35. **heredity**
36. C
37. B
38. D
39. C
40. B
41. B
42. **heat**
43. **it creates an identical copy of the DNA.**
44. C
45. B
46. **protons**
47. C
48. B
49. D
50. D

Section 4: Mathematical Reasoning

1. **C**

2. **A**

3. **$1,680**

4. **B**

5. **average**

6. **A**

7. **D**

8. **66**

9. **B**

10. **D**

11. **2/3**

12. **(–6, 0)**

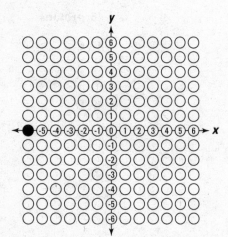

13. **D**

14. **C**

15. **A**

16. **1,140**

17. **(6, 6)**

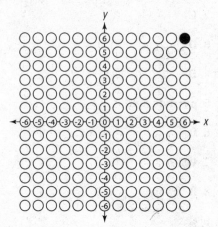

18. **B**

19. **C**

20. **D**

21. **A**

22. **C**

23. **B**

24. **C**

25. **320**

26. **multiplication**

27. **D**

28. **7:1**

29. **5**

30. **D**

31. **$78.50**

32. **$3.20**

33. **D**

34. **D**

35. **A**

36. **12**

37. **D**

38. **4.48**

39. **D**

40. **A**

41. **(0, 5)**

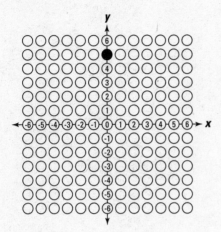

42. **D**

43. **B**

44. **D**

45. **3 hours**

46. **D**

47. **A**

48. **C**

49. **A**

50. **C**

Index

• *W* •

Notes

Notes

Notes

About the Authors

Murray Shukyn is a graduate of the University of Toronto with professional qualifications as a teacher at the elementary and secondary levels, including special education. He has taught at the elementary, secondary, and university levels and developed training programs for adult learners in the coffee and foodservice industries. During his extensive career, spanning more than 30 years, he has taught professional development programs for educators and is acknowledged as a Canadian leader in the field of alternative education. He was instrumental in the creation of such innovative programs for the Toronto Board of Education as SEED, Learnxs, Subway Academy, SOLE, and ACE. In 1995, he became Associate Director of the Training Renewal Foundation, which introduced the GED in the province of Ontario. As a consultant to government, media, and public relations companies, he has coauthored numerous textbooks and magazine and periodical articles with Achim Krull and coauthored several books to prepare adults to take the GED test with Dale Shuttleworth.

Dale E. Shuttleworth's professional career as a community educator has included experience as a teacher, school-community worker, consultant, principal, coordinator, school superintendent, university course director, and executive director. He has been influential in policy development provincially, nationally, and internationally. He has been a speaker and resource leader throughout Canada and the United States and in Europe, Africa, and Asia. He has served as an expert/consultant to the Organization for Economic Cooperation and Development (OCED) in Paris. He is the author of more than 120 articles in books, journals, and periodicals. His publications include *Enterprise Learning in Action* (Routledge), *How to Prepare for the GED* (Barron's), *School Management in Transition* (Routledge), *The GED For Dummies* (Wiley), *Schooling for Life* (University of Toronto Press), *Playing Fast & Loose* (Campaign for Public Education), and *CliffsNotes GED Cram Plan* (Wiley).

Achim K. Krull, BA, MAT, is a graduate of the University of Toronto, with specialist qualifications in history and geography. He has taught at both the high-school and adult education level, most recently preparing young adults for entry into apprenticeship programs. He worked for many years in the academic alternative schools of the Toronto District School Board, as administrator/curriculum leader of Subway Academy One and cofounder of SOLE. He has written textbooks, teachers' guides, and a large variety of other learning materials with Murray Shukyn, including scripts for educational television programs, as well as writing for newspapers and magazines.

Publisher's Acknowledgments

Acquisitions Editor: Erin Calligan Mooney

Senior Project Editor: Alissa Schwipps

Copy Editor: Jennette ElNaggar

Technical Editor: Sonia Chaumette

Project Coordinator: Patrick Redmond

Cover Image: ©iStockphoto.com/Marvelens

Apple & Mac

iPad For Dummies,
5th Edition
978-1-118-49823-1

iPhone 5 For Dummies,
6th Edition
978-1-118-35201-4

MacBook For Dummies,
4th Edition
978-1-118-20920-2

OS X Mountain Lion
For Dummies
978-1-118-39418-2

Blogging & Social Media

Facebook For Dummies,
4th Edition
978-1-118-09562-1

Mom Blogging
For Dummies
978-1-118-03843-7

Pinterest For Dummies
978-1-118-32800-2

WordPress For Dummies,
5th Edition
978-1-118-38318-6

Business

Commodities For Dummies,
2nd Edition
978-1-118-01687-9

Investing For Dummies,
6th Edition
978-0-470-90545-6

Personal Finance
For Dummies, 7th Edition
978-1-118-11785-9

QuickBooks 2013
For Dummies
978-1-118-35641-8

Small Business Marketing
Kit For Dummies,
3rd Edition
978-1-118-31183-7

Careers

Job Interviews
For Dummies, 4th Edition
978-1-118-11290-8

Job Searching with
Social Media
For Dummies
978-0-470-93072-4

Personal Branding
For Dummies
978-1-118-11792-7

Resumes For Dummies,
6th Edition
978-0-470-87361-8

Success as a Mediator
For Dummies
978-1-118-07862-4

Diet & Nutrition

Belly Fat Diet For Dummies
978-1-118-34585-6

Eating Clean For Dummies
978-1-118-00013-7

Nutrition For Dummies,
5th Edition
978-0-470-93231-5

Digital Photography

Digital Photography
For Dummies,
7th Edition
978-1-118-09203-3

Digital SLR Cameras &
Photography For Dummies,
4th Edition
978-1-118-14489-3

Photoshop Elements 11
For Dummies
978-1-118-40821-6

Gardening

Herb Gardening
For Dummies, 2nd Edition
978-0-470-61778-6

Vegetable Gardening
For Dummies, 2nd Edition
978-0-470-49870-5

Health

Anti-Inflammation Diet
For Dummies
978-1-118-02381-5

Diabetes For Dummies,
3rd Edition
978-0-470-27086-8

Living Paleo For Dummies
978-1-118-29405-5

Hobbies

Beekeeping
For Dummies
978-0-470-43065-1

eBay For Dummies,
7th Edition
978-1-118-09806-6

Raising Chickens
For Dummies
978-0-470-46544-8

Wine For Dummies,
5th Edition
978-1-118-28872-6

Writing Young Adult Fiction
For Dummies
978-0-470-94954-2

Language &
Foreign Language

500 Spanish Verbs
For Dummies
978-1-118-02382-2

English Grammar
For Dummies, 2nd Edition
978-0-470-54664-2

French All-in One
For Dummies
978-1-118-22815-9

German Essentials
For Dummies
978-1-118-18422-6

Italian For Dummies,
2nd Edition
978-1-118-00465-4

Available in print and e-book formats.

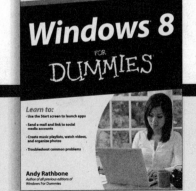

Math & Science

Algebra I For Dummies,
2nd Edition
978-0-470-55964-2

Anatomy and Physiology
For Dummies,
2nd Edition
978-0-470-92326-9

Astronomy For Dummies,
3rd Edition
978-1-118-37697-3

Biology For Dummies,
2nd Edition
978-0-470-59875-7

Chemistry For Dummies,
2nd Edition
978-1-1180-0730-3

Pre-Algebra Essentials
For Dummies
978-0-470-61838-7

Microsoft Office

Excel 2013 For Dummies
978-1-118-51012-4

Office 2013 All-in-One
For Dummies
978-1-118-51636-2

PowerPoint 2013
For Dummies
978-1-118-50253-2

Word 2013 For Dummies
978-1-118-49123-2

Music

Blues Harmonica
For Dummies
978-1-118-25269-7

Guitar For Dummies,
3rd Edition
978-1-118-11554-1

iPod & iTunes
For Dummies,
10th Edition
978-1-118-50864-0

Programming

Android Application
Development For Dummies,
2nd Edition
978-1-118-38710-8

iOS 6 Application
Development For Dummies
978-1-118-50880-0

Java For Dummies,
5th Edition
978-0-470-37173-2

Religion & Inspiration

The Bible For Dummies
978-0-7645-5296-0

Buddhism For Dummies,
2nd Edition
978-1-118-02379-2

Catholicism For Dummies,
2nd Edition
978-1-118-07778-8

Self-Help & Relationships

Bipolar Disorder
For Dummies,
2nd Edition
978-1-118-33882-7

Meditation For Dummies,
3rd Edition
978-1-118-29144-3

Seniors

Computers For Seniors
For Dummies,
3rd Edition
978-1-118-11553-4

iPad For Seniors
For Dummies,
5th Edition
978-1-118-49708-1

Social Security
For Dummies
978-1-118-20573-0

Smartphones & Tablets

Android Phones
For Dummies
978-1-118-16952-0

Kindle Fire HD
For Dummies
978-1-118-42223-6

NOOK HD For Dummies,
Portable Edition
978-1-118-39498-4

Surface For Dummies
978-1-118-49634-3

Test Prep

ACT For Dummies,
5th Edition
978-1-118-01259-8

ASVAB For Dummies,
3rd Edition
978-0-470-63760-9

GRE For Dummies,
7th Edition
978-0-470-88921-3

Officer Candidate Tests,
For Dummies
978-0-470-59876-4

Physician's Assistant Exam
For Dummies
978-1-118-11556-5

Series 7 Exam
For Dummies
978-0-470-09932-2

Windows 8

Windows 8 For Dummies
978-1-118-13461-0

Windows 8 For Dummies,
Book + DVD Bundle
978-1-118-27167-4

Windows 8 All-in-One
For Dummies
978-1-118-11920-4

e Available in print and e-book formats.

Take Dummies with you everywhere you go!

Whether you're excited about e-books, want more from the web, must have your mobile apps, or swept up in social media, Dummies makes everything easier .